The Trust Paradigm

Develop Trusting Client Relationships To Improve Your Career And Life

By Andy Fry

Vantage Point Publishing

The Trust Paradigm: Develop Trusting Relationships To Improve Your Career And Life

Published by Vantage Point Publishing, Vantage Point Digital Media, LLC
16211 N. Scottsdale Rd, Unit A6A #425, Scottsdale, AZ, 85254

First Published in 2020 by Vantage Point Publishing, Vantage Point Digital Media, LLC

https://www.theconsultingplaybook.com

For permission to use excerpts contact:
Andy Fry at 401-321-2468, info@quantasconsulting.com, https://www.theconsultingplaybook.com

Edited by Chantel Hamilton, Afterwords Communications
Cover and design by pro_ebookcovers

First Edition
ISBN: 978-0-9995354-1-7

This book is not endorsed, supported or written by any other person than the author.

TABLE OF CONTENTS

Introduction

"Trustful people are the pure at heart, as they are moved by the zeal of their own trustworthiness." -Criss Jami

A number of years ago, while working for a new consulting client, I received a call from another company that I had worked with on multiple occasions. They were located in Canada and had extensive operations in the oil and gas sector. With the price of oil dropping, they had undergone a large number of layoffs. It was December, and the engineering group needed some help to wrap up some projects and do some year-end reporting.

When I told the current client's Project Manager, who was named Sam, that I planned to serve both companies at the same time over the next few weeks, I didn't expect the hostile response I received:

Sam said, "No, you're under contract to us, and we're not allowing you to leave to help another company".

Ouch.

We eventually figured out a balance of sorts, but Sam wasn't happy about it, and I could tell he was relieved when I wrapped up with the Canadian client. Maybe I would've forgotten about it altogether, but six months later, it happened again.

This time, the Canadian company was performing a mid-year analysis, and they invited me back to help. I struggled with having to approach Sam again. Internally, I questioned why, after 18 years of consulting experience, I needed to go through a begging process to ask to help another client. Shouldn't my dedication and the results speak for themselves? After all, Sam and his company were getting everything that we had agreed to. The project was on schedule, and I had taken on additional work to help out in other areas that needed assistance. I wanted to see them successful, and I was doing everything I could to provide my advice and skills, both when requested and when I noticed opportunities for improvement.

Wasn't about the Project

This is when I realized that none of this had anything to do with the project.

The real problem was that **Sam did not trust me.** Or perhaps, he didn't trust consultants in general. Maybe he didn't trust his own group to get work done and keep the project moving while I was gone. Maybe Sam didn't trust his bosses to take responsibility for any issues that may have occurred.

Another realization came to me soon after: **I didn't trust Sam either.** I felt he did not have my consulting career in mind when he made those rigid decisions. He was very nearsighted not considering that the company may need my help sometime in the future after my contract was completed and being flexible might help foster a longer-term relationship.

Maybe it sounds odd that a consultant should have to trust a client. We spend so much of our time trying to get others to trust *us*. Does it even need to go both ways? **I've learned that it does.** Trusting the client allows a consultant to deliver better service and provide much better results. This comes from knowing that there is a purpose and meaning to the work you are performing and that you are part of the solution, not just a tool to do the work.

Finally, a third realization: **Neither Sam nor I trusted ourselves** enough to get the job done. This lack of trust we both may have felt with ourselves caused internal conflict that resulted in outward anxiety and conflict. For Sam and his company, if they trusted themselves, they would have realized they were in a safe situation that could allow a consultant to not be onsite for a week. If I trusted myself, I would have made it clear to Sam right away that they were safe. I would have resolved the issue in the first conversation. When we trust our abilities, capabilities, and skills, we feel little conflict. When we distrust ourselves, we feel stress and conflict.

This experience was a perfect example of trust and distrust. One company felt comfortable to call me and ask for my help when they really required it. They felt comfortable being flexible to work around my schedule as well as my other contractual obligations. They felt comfortable enough and trusted me enough to ask me to come back to help with their mid-year reviews.

On the other end of the spectrum, the other client viewed the relationship very transactionally. They were rigid and inflexible and only willing to give when they realized they didn't have any other choice.

Can you guess which company I still have a strong, productive, profitable relationship with?

Trust Goes Three Ways

When I talk to even seasoned and experienced consultants about how important trust is, many of them respond with a very puzzled look. This may be because most of us are not taught that trust is even a component of our work, let alone that such a critical factor to our careers. We take it for granted until it's gone.

We trust that our clients will pay us and that they'll take our advice.

Our clients trust that we know what we are talking about and that we will get them results.

We trust ourselves to support, manage, and defend ourselves. We trust that we know what we're doing to better our lives as well as those that personally depend on us.

Once I started to explain to the other consultants that all the privileges we receive are based on if and how much

our client trusts us, how we trust our client, and even
how we trust ourselves, they typically begin to agree.

Three-Way Trust: The Trust Relationship

The concept of three-way trust--how we trust others,
how others trust us, and how we trust ourselves--is like a
triangle.

The design of a triangle makes it one of the strongest and
most stable structures, allowing them to be secure,
unwavering and handle stress. The equilateral triangle is
structurally the strongest type of triangle, for obvious
reasons. Equal angles and vectors naturally resist
gravitational and lateral forces equally in all directions.

When it comes to trust, each of the three directions of
trust represent one side of the triangle;

- How the client trusts us
- How we trust the client
- How we trust ourselves

Figure 1

When pressure is applied to a relationship or situation and when trust is strong across all three directions the pressure is spread equally across the trust that has been built and nurtured, such as figure 3 below.

Figure 2

Figure 3

A triangle that is not equal in nature will feel stable when stress and pressure is lacking. As seen below in figure 5, the stress of the pressure is not evenly distributed resulting in strain on the relationship.

Figure 4

Figure 5

A relationship that is significantly lacking trust in an area has exaggerated trust angles resulting in a very unstable relationship. This relationship is built on a weak foundation and can be destroyed or fall over with a small amount of stress and pressure as can be seen in figure 7.

Figure 6

Figure 7

As you can see in the above images the relationship may not show signs of instability while there is a lack of stress, however more pressure could be sustained if the client had more trust in us. This is why some relationships struggle. As pressure increases the area of weakness almost always becomes apparent as stress. As consultants, pressure and stress is a part of our careers. In fact, it is one of the reasons our clients hire us to begin with. It is imperative that we develop strong trust across each angle of trust.

In reality most relationships will not have equivalent amounts of trust as not all parties have the same experience, awareness and risk tolerance. Also, trust is dynamic and is constantly changing. This is why most of us are operating with a triangle that will change shape in our relationships. For instance, a client may not have much trust at the beginning of a project but may develop more trust as the project continues. At the same time a consultant may lose trust in a client as a project continues, due to various factors such as late payment, inconsistency and or being the target of unnecessary conflict.

When trust grows equally each side of the triangle also grows. A large equilateral triangle can sustain a lot of pressure. This is why working to develop each component of trust is important to the success of a consultant. Keeping in mind this concept, a consultant can gauge what level of trust exists in a relationship and work to develop the components of trust that are not as strong as other components.

Why Not Just Reduce Stress?

Another approach to dealing with pressure and strain on our trust is to reduce the other factor, which is stress. This is the approach many people take. Rather than developing trust, they do things to reduce stress. Positive stress such as added responsibilities, new opportunities or professional growth can generate negative stress such questioning our own abilities, being responsible for others or having to develop deeper client relationships. The negative stress puts pressure on each angle of trust as you are developing these new roles and skills.

Mediocre individuals learn that to limit the impact on trust they reduce negative stress. They often do this by accepting less responsibilities and opportunities. Unfortunately, this approach is why most people never come close to experiencing their full potential.

Of course, we need to reduce actions that directly cause negative stress which results in a limit to our development. However, we also need to develop skills to take advantage of positive stress, like new opportunities. This is done by increasing the skills related to the four components of trust.

Components of Trust

Let's dig into trust a little more. We know that trust goes three ways, and it is built using four components: credibility, authenticity, reliability, and empathy.

Credibility:
When someone believes that you have the particular ability and skills to know or do something.

Authenticity:
When someone else believes that you are acting in a manner that is true, real, and genuine.

Reliability:
When someone believes that you act in a manner that is consistent to what they expect, and you do what you say you will.

Empathy:
When others believe that you can understand and share their feelings and have their best interest in mind.

When someone distrusts someone else, that person is missing one or more of these four components. They may have outright violated the rules regarding that component, or they may have not yet earned that component. In some cases, one of the individuals may have been affected by prior experiences and the other individual has to overcome that preconception.

In my example, Sam may have felt that I was unreliable to them since I wanted to help another client. Negative past experiences may have taught Sam that consultants are unreliable when they are off site resulting in him not trusting me. He also may have felt I was violating his definition of authenticity as many clients expect that a consultant is 100% dedicated to them and only them. Sam also showed very little empathy for me and my commitments and relationships with others. He may have also downplayed my competence as any consultant with a high level of skills and ability would be in demand by other clients.

Regardless of the reasons, Sam caused me to not trust him which resulted in a more strained relationship between us and ultimately his organization. On a positive note, out of that strained relationship came this book.

How to Read This Book

This book is designed in four major sections. The first focusing on how credibility affects trust. The second section focuses on authenticity. The third section focuses on reliability and the fourth on empathy.

Each section of the book is made up of three chapters. The first chapter focuses on my experiences and what I've seen throughout my career relating to trust. The second chapter of each section focuses on research and scientific information related to that component. In the third chapter of each section, we'll discuss how you can make changes to build trust in regard to that specific component.

High trust in others allows us to have a relaxed, comfortable, and rewarding experience as a consultant. When others have high trust in us, it provides us with privileges that better our careers and our day-to-day experiences. Finally, having high trust in ourselves allows us to spend energy on positive growth opportunities rather than questioning the decisions that we've made and being overly self-critical.

The book is grounded on the lessons and experiences from decades of consulting. It is based on what a consultant will participate in and witness on a daily basis with their clients and themselves. Although focused on consulting, this advice can be applied to our personal and professional lives.

Trust Exercise

Use the information in this book to determine why you trust or don't trust someone. When you trust another person ask yourself, "What does that person do or how do they behave that builds trust?" Use the four components of trust to better identify the behavior, actions and characteristics of the person. This will help you improve your ability in identifying trust building actions and qualities.

Perform the same steps for trusting relationships where others trust you. Ask yourself "What do I do and how do I behave that builds trust with my client?" You can replace the word client with another person but perform the steps to better recognize what you excel at in the areas of trust.

Do the same exercise that questions what you do to build trust in yourself. Recognize actions that you undertake where you build confidence and where you would trust yourself to take on activities in the future.

The purpose of this exercise is two-fold. First it helps you recognize the components of trust in your relationships. It also allows you to better identify when trust components exist, and this will be the building block to notice when trust components are missing. I feel it is easier to recognize when an ability is missing by comparing it to situations when the skill exists.

Once you are comfortable with recognizing areas where trust exists perform the same review in situations where trust does not exist. For instance, if you have lost trust in another person, let's say another consultant, ask yourself "What have they done or not done that violated the components of trust?" Use the detailed information in each chapter to recognize what occurred that damaged trust.

By performing these steps, you will be better prepared to recognize trust building or trust damaging behavior. You will recognize the actions that you are taking to earn trust. Also, you will be able to use this information to coach and train others or yourself to develop the deficient skills.

There are countless relationships that have been discarded due to lack of trust. However, many of those connections could have been saved and converted to rewarding and successful relationships. Use the information in this book to develop gratifying and satisfying relationships and interactions.

For bonus material please visit:
https://theconsultingplaybook.com/bonus

Who is this Book For?

This book is written for those that want to develop the skills to improve trust. If your intent is to earn more privileges or opportunities, then this book is meant for you. If you are someone who has avoided opportunities and responsibilities to reduce stress but now want to improve then please apply the lessons in this book to develop your trust skills. Privileges and opportunities come with responsibility and a large part of that responsibility is to develop the components related to trust.

The ultimate goal of every consultant should be to become a trusted advisor to their clients. The time is now to develop these skills. I strongly believe that skills and awareness related to trust are some of the most important talents that drive success yet are also some of the most underdeveloped.

So for those that want to develop, grow and improve.....let's get to it!

Section 1: Credibility

Chapter 1: Credibility and Trust

"Commitment and credibility go hand in hand."
-Zbigniew Brzezinski

What We Think Credibility Is

Many years ago, when I worked for Oracle, I was in a training course. Each consultant was to introduce themselves. One gentleman stood up and gave his name. After he stated his name, he said, "And I'm a CA (Chartered Accountant)." The entire room started laughing as almost every person in that room was a designated accountant.

What this experience showed was that this gentleman had frequently indicated his designation when he introduced himself to others to identify that he was credible. The reason that everybody laughed at the training session was that the designation didn't deem him to be credible in that particular environment. Not only was almost everyone in the room a designated accountant, this was an information technology company. Therefore, he was no more credible than anyone else right out of the gate.

I remember once receiving a business card from another consultant. He had a number of initials after his name that were not familiar to me. When I asked what those initials meant, the gentleman responded back, seemingly quite annoyed. This was a situation where the initials did not provide credibility as they were not related in any way to our industry.

It doesn't mean that the gentleman didn't have qualified skills or that the knowledge gained through those designations or certifications wasn't valuable. What it meant was that he would have to show his credibility in other ways as the initials themselves didn't tell me or anyone else unfamiliar with them what they meant.

Many of us base credibility on external indicators. Designations and degrees as well as where we went to school often trigger thoughts in our mind that someone is more credible or less credible than someone else. In consulting it can be common that a consultant who arrives at a client site from a prestigious firm will be viewed as more credible than a consultant coming from a lesser known firm. This is because the client and others may hold value in the prestigious firm's name and history. However, it is just as common that over time the consultant from the lesser known firm will end up with the same level of credibility or surpasses the credibility of the other consultant. This is because the consultant from the more prestigious firm is being graded on an external factor for their credibility and not credibility that they earned on their own.

Credibility is required when we need others to trust us. In fact, we don't question the credibility of someone until we need to trust them when their decisions or actions have a resulting consequence to us.

Do we question the credibility of a consultant that we've never heard of? Of course not. Do we question the credibility of another consultant that we may have heard of but who does not impact us? No.

We don't spend any time thinking about their credibility because it doesn't impact us... until it does.

What Credibility Actually Is

Credibility is three different things, depending on the circumstances:

Initial Credibility
Initial credibility is the credibility a consultant has when they first interact with a client. In most cases, initial credibility is granted when the consultant, speaker, or presenter first interacts with their clients.

I worked for a client where a new consultant was brought in. His name was Derek, and his first interaction with us was the Monday morning status meeting. When the project manager introduced Derek, she asked him to tell the team a little bit about himself. When he began to speak, you could clearly see he was missing a front tooth. My initial thought was, *Where did they find this guy?*

It was quite some time later after I got to know him that I asked him about his missing tooth. He laughed and said the night before, he was playing hockey and took a stick in the face that knocked his tooth out. There was no other damage to his face, so no one saw anything other than the missing tooth.

His initial credibility was slightly less because of the missing tooth. Oddly enough, this project was in Edmonton, Alberta. Had he introduced himself and said, "Hey everybody, just to let you know, I took the stick in the face last night while playing hockey, and I lost my tooth," he would have gained initial credibility due to their understanding of the game of hockey.

A similar situation occurred with another consultant that I worked with whose name was Darcy. Darcy was on a fishing trip in Alaska and showed up in shorts and sandals to his flight. When he arrived in Juneau, he received a call saying that a client in Juneau wanted him to stop by and do a quick presentation. Darcy knew the material he was going to present on very well so that wasn't an issue. The issue was the fact that he looked like he was going fishing.

When he showed up to the client site and walked into the meeting room, he immediately told everyone that he was in Juneau for a fishing weekend but stopped by to see them to share some information. The initial credibility ranked very high for Darcy because they understood why he was dressed as he was and that he was taking time out of his day to present to them.

Transactional Credibility

Transactional credibility is the credibility that is gained as the consultant is executing their work. It can be gained or lost throughout the engagement. If you hear a client say, "We lost trust in them," then they are saying that the transactional credibility was so low, it affected the trust gained from any initial credibility. While building transactional credibility, an opportunity to start balancing the components of trust presents itself.

Terminal Credibility

Terminal credibility is the credibility that is left with the client at the end of an engagement. Your goal should be to have high terminal credibility. This allows you to have repeat business, referrals, and an overall better relationship with your clients. However, quite often many consultants leave with very low terminal credibility as they may have begun to lose credibility at the end of the transaction. Unfortunately, some consultants want to get out of the client site before the house of cards they built comes falling down. This is also why so many companies value client satisfaction surveys after a service has been provided. The feedback on the survey indicates the level of terminal credibility and provides opportunities for improvement.

Understanding these phases of credibility is important for consultants because too often, consultants and even clients view credibility as one specific measurement. I've often seen consultants show up day one and have very high initial credibility. They look good, they've gained the client's trust in some manner, and they have what is perceived as expertise. But over time, they lose credibility by not engaging with their clients, having transactional challenges that are not resolved, and often they do not invest in trust related activities throughout the engagement.

Why Credibility Is Important for Consultants

Credibility is based primarily on expectations. Remember, credibility is what others believe that we can do. Often people define credibility as, "doing what you say you can do." In simple terms, that is correct. However, our relationships with our clients are frequently more complicated. There are implied and expected abilities that our clients have. If our clients believe we have the skills and abilities in a particular area, then in their eyes, we are credible in those skills. However, we can lose credibility by not meeting the expectations of our clients whether or not we have those skills or not.

Likewise, if you have a set of skills, experience, and abilities but your client does not believe you do, then you can create credibility by exceeding the expectations of your client.

We Recognize Credibility in Others

The nature of consulting puts consultants in positions where we work with people and clients with varying degrees of credibility, experience, and commitment. We can work with superstar people who dwarf our abilities, and we can also work with people that are insecure in their abilities and take this out on others they collaborate with.

I once worked for a client who had a senior manager who was in way over his head in his job. He lacked many of the skills required for his position. He would overcompensate for his lack of knowledge by trying to control more of the procedures. This put his staff in a position where they were not able to make decisions. In fact, many of them were not able to execute their jobs properly as he was constantly meddling in their roles. Due to his anxieties, he would limit the ability of developers and programmers, which did not allow them to fully do their jobs.

What resulted was a lack of trust from all of the individuals who worked for him. People began to question the decision-making abilities of his managers. His subordinates wondered how he could get away with these steps without upper management knowing.

This type of incompetence places people in a position of losing trust due to this lack of credibility.

Others Recognize Credibility in Us

For most consultants we must articulate a set of skills and abilities to our clients. When we are explaining what skills we have, we are using a subjective manner of explanation. I'm a CPA and a PMP, which indicates that I have skills in accounting and project management. However, there are thousands of CPAs and thousands of

PMPs, and we all have different levels of skills in each of those areas.

When we are explaining skills that aren't measured with credentials, many people will use a grading system to describe the level of our skills. Often a measurement such as 0 to 5 is used, with 0 representing not knowing anything about the subject and 5 representing being an expert. A client's measurement may be much different than that of a consultant's. When we are selling our capabilities to others, there is danger in under or over selling our skills.

We Recognize Credibility in Ourselves

In regard to our own credibility, we can also lose trust in ourselves affecting our confidence level. Everyone questions their ability from time to time. This is common, and it's just part of being a human. However, we can lose trust in ourselves and our confidence when we don't live up to our potential. Most people seldom regret putting in an effort and trying something new. However, regret comes from not accomplishing the things that we felt we were capable of.

Each time we miss the mark because we're not living up to our potential, this chips away at our trust in ourselves. This is the equivalent of someone constantly doing mediocre things around us until we finally have the expectation that the next task, they complete will also be mediocre. The challenge here is that we are the one executing the task and also receiving the benefit of the task.

Not living up to our potential is more than just being busy or falling short once in a while. This is when a systemic problem occurs when we are unable to get the most out of ourselves or even come close to the expectations, we have in ourselves. It's important to note I'm not advocating perfection. This is about getting the most out of our lives and the skills that we've developed.

When we lose trust in regard to credibility in ourselves, we lose confidence. When we lose confidence in ourselves, others can usually notice it. One of the biggest downsides of losing confidence in yourself is that the client is expecting and relying on their consultants to be confident. Again, consultants don't need to know every answer, but we need to be confident in what we're delivering. When we lose trust in ourselves, that confidence could be broken. It affects all areas of consulting and can negatively affect our lives.

Personal Responsibility

Throughout this book there is an underlying value that is associated to each skill and component of trust. That value is personal responsibility. To be successful in any endeavor each individual must take personal responsibility for their progress. This includes developing and maintaining the skills related to trust. You need to take responsibility for your actions, thoughts and behavior. As you continue to read this book keep in mind your personal responsibility as you learn the concepts and skills discussed throughout these chapters.

Chapter 2: What the Experts Say About Credibility

"The more you are willing to accept responsibility for your actions, the more credibility you will have."
-Brian Koslow

As a consultant, we know that you get paid to do your work, and you're not there to work for free. However, I have seen consultants lose tremendous amounts of credibility when they make a statement like, "I'll do any work that you ask me as long as you pay me for it." This implies to the client that you're only there for money and for no one else's best interest except your own.

Those who are focused on their own interests are called opportunistic by researchers, Machiavellian by psychologists, and selfish by children. Opportunistic people view everyone they come in contact with as a tool for them to use to get what they want. Now I am not suggesting that we shouldn't have goals or have our needs met. But opportunists are *only* focused on their own goals with little to no concern on how their actions or objectives impact of others. Opportunists view other people as a mode to achieve their objectives and they often move on with no remorse on the damage they've created once their goals have been met.

In his book *Who Cares*, Roger Fritz describes deceivers as opportunists. He also defines them as people who:

- Don't deliver what they promise
- Need protection
- Deny, delay, destroy
- Are not appreciative
- Cover up
- Spin the truth
- Put themselves first
- Encourage confusion

You might read that list and think that no one could have all of those characteristics. In my experience, opportunists or deceivers do have these characteristics. I'm not referring to people who take advantage of an opportunity. If a business or economic situation occurs that is advantageous to someone, then they should use that advantage. What this scenario is talking about is exploiting other people.

In the book *Credibility*, James M. Kouzes and Barry Z Posner say that "credible leaders invite others to elaborate their own perspectives which are often quite different and incompatible. These opposing ideas and positions challenge or provoke people's thinking. Appreciating diversity allows the controversy to stimulate innovative thinking and encourage actively searching for new information."

Consultants often believe that it is their job to have all the information. At times we are there to solve a specific problem, and clients bring us in for our specific expertise. Often though the issue is more in-depth, and we need the client to be involved with the problem-solving approach as well as the implementation of any solution. Getting the client's perspective helps ensure that the decisions that are made are more successful.

In the book *Achieving Credibility*, James M. Kouzes compares credibility to credit. This comparison is creative, as both words have the same root word of "credo." Kouzes states that "people must ask of the creditworthiness of those that we might follow." Of course, he is not literally describing the financial creditworthiness, although that may be the case in some situations. He is explaining that credibility is built up from doing investments over time, such as doing what we say we can, developing the skills required for our roles, and other ways of building credibility. Once we develop and demonstrate those investments then others deem us to be credible.

Communication Effectiveness

Studies have shown that the effectiveness of communication can be based on how credible the listeners believe the speaker is. The study conducted by Hovland, Lumsdaine, and Sheffield had two speakers, one who was of trustworthy character and the other who was of untrustworthy character. One finding of the study was that over time, participants had less of a recall of the source of the material when the communication was from an untrusted source.

Why is connecting the source of information important for consultants? Because you want to be connected to the material that you're presenting to your client. Have you ever told a story or educated people on something and then later someone else got credit for that information? It might be a bit infuriating when you're among friends talking about some sports information or some news that occurred. But as a consultant, this is your livelihood. To be connected to that information brings an immediate recall to you, and therefore, you are likely to be called back again to do more work by that client or to clarify things if they have questions. Being credible helps connect that information to you.

Source Credibility

According to the Credibility Institute, source credibility "is an established theory that explains how communication's persuasiveness is affected by the perceived credibility of the source of the communication. The credibility of all communication, regardless of format, has been found to be heavily influenced by the perceived credibility of the source of that communication."

This is based on three conditions:

1. Trustworthiness
2. Expertise or competence
3. Attractiveness, appeal, or enthusiasm

To clarify what attractiveness or appeal means, it is how energetic or enthusiastic consultants are when delivering their message. We have all seen a message that is delivered where the consultant or speaker is clearly competent and has expertise, but their lack of enthusiasm kills the message.

Message Credibility

Message credibility is how items such as content, language, and presentation skills can impact the believability of the information. This is similar to source credibility, however message credibility focuses on the content or skills related to delivering a message. "In some situations where little information is available about the source of a message, people tend to turn to message cues in making credibility judgments".

I once was in a hockey coaching course. There was a speaker who was to present on developing speed and fitness during the off season. You could clearly see that the speaker was very knowledgeable in her field. One issue was that she would routinely use the wrong terms when it came to hockey. For instance, she used the term "rotation," when in hockey we use the term "shift." Now these were minor errors when delivering content, however it did put those listening to the message in a position where they may have questioned her information.

People may not take time to ask themselves why they may be questioning the information when errors in communication occur. "Rather, people often rely on mental shortcuts to judgmental rules (or heuristics), which have evolved as generalizations in their knowledge base and have thus been refined through the course of their experience." People may not be aware of how their judgement rules will affect how they determine a message to be credible or not credible. "Cues that trigger heuristics can either be embedded in a message or internally located within people's cognition"

This is why some conversations go off the rails when someone misspeaks causing others to capitalize on the error. They use that error to their advantage and challenge the validity of all of the content. This is where the term throwing the baby out with the bathwater comes from. The term means removing something valuable during the process of removing something of no value.

Chapter 3: How to Become More Credible

"I knew credibility would come only in time through earnest performances." -Dwayne Johnson

Credibility can be summed up with another word which is belief. When someone considers you credible, they are stating, "I believe in you." Do you notice how that is more than just saying, "I believe you have the skills," or, "I believe you know what you are saying"? It is more because credibility includes your competence and analytical skills. It is more than just specific skills.

In Micheal Burt's book, *Person of Interest*, he tells us that people are looking for those that believe in the same thing. His approach includes the following steps:

1. Start with what you believe
2. Why you believe it
3. What is it that you really do
4. What makes you different from all others
5. List all the people you have done it for
6. Ask them, what piques your interest
7. Ask, if we believe the same thing, then what would stop us from doing business together

Combinations of this approach work while you are at the client site delivering your services. Reminding the client of what you believe in reinforces them with your purpose of being their consultant. Your credibility will shoot through the roof when your beliefs are in line with your client's beliefs. A word of warning though is that you can't fake this. If you are telling the client a line of bull just to make yourself look like you are singing from their hymn book, you will be found out. If this happens, your credibility could be permanently damaged with that client. You are better off not stating your beliefs if your beliefs are not in sync with your clients.

My recommendation though is to constantly be searching for clients whose beliefs are in sync with yours. This is the purpose of the explanation of services and why being relational upfront is much better than being transactional.

17 Ways to Become More Credible

1. Live your values and purpose

In James M. Kouzes and Barry Z. Posner's book named *Credibility: How Leaders Gain and Lose It, Why People Demand It*, the authors refer to credibility and leadership. They say that it can be built by having common values and purpose. They write: "In any event, constituents take us most seriously when all of the supporting organizational mechanisms reinforce our individual commitments to common values and purpose."

What this means as a consultant who is coming in and making changes in a client's organization is to understand the client's values and purpose of making these changes. Purpose is more than just the requirements. A purpose is the overall reason an

organization or individual is taking on a change. Some people will refer to this as their *why*. However, I don't like to use the word *why* as it implies questioning and usually puts people in a defensive mode. Often when someone asks a company, "Why are you doing this?" the answer is vague and unclear. When we ask questions like, "What is the overall purpose of making these changes?" people tend not to take it personally.
Now many consultants will say, "I have no control over the purpose for the changes of an organization." You are absolutely correct. However, knowing and understanding the purpose helps you better support your clients and also better aligns your values with theirs.

This also means that as a consultant you can take a leadership role in the area that you are to deliver knowing the purpose of these changes. Those who support military organizations will often use phrases like, "They support the mission," which might be one of the nicest things that could be said to someone who is working for an organization that supports the military. It means we trust them, and we know they're on our team. It doesn't mean they won't get angry or frustrated with you, or that you won't make mistakes. But it means you're on their team, and it might be the highest form of respect I've heard when someone in the military is referring to a civilian. I can feel the love and energy produced when that statement is made as it is coming from the speaker's heart because it aligns with their values.

2. Do what you say you will

A big part of credibility is doing what you say you will. This also falls into reliability, however consultants can often lose a lot of credibility when they just don't do what they say they will. What we need to do as a consultant is understand the timelines that are expected and not over promise. It's okay to over promise if you can deliver, but to over promise and underdeliver is the worst thing a consultant can do.

Our clients won't forget what we promised to do, so don't think that over time they'll just forget the promises you made, and they'll let you slide. Remember, *you* work for *them*.

3. Make eye contact

I knew a couple of acquaintances where one of the men did not trust the other man because he would never make eye contact. He was always thrown off by the fact that the guy would never look him in the eye when he talked. I thought possibly this is just being blown out of proportion until I had a talk with the gentleman, and I realized there was no connection. He would talk but look elsewhere and often have the appearance of not even being engaged with the conversation.

To generate credibility, make sure you're making eye contact. You shouldn't stare at people. One trick is to look from one eye to the other. Not quickly, just look at one eye for a few moments and then look at the other eye.

Eye contact is critical for the success of a consultant. Clients will feel they cannot trust you if you cannot make eye contact with them.

4. Listen intently

Listening might be the most important skill of a consultant, yet most people are not taught how to listen properly. Often, we are trying to think of our next response, and other times we're doing completely different things in our minds. Other times we are distracted as we use technical devices while we should be listening. It's important to be engaged when we listen and don't try to respond in your head. One trick is to let the other person make their points. If you want to write down notes to remind you how you can respond, that's fine, but you must be listening to what they're saying.

In North America people have different ways of communicating. Some people raise the problem at the beginning of their statement. Others give analogies, while others speak in a very passive mode, hoping for you to come to the conclusion that they want. Others may even speak in a very explicit mode where they just present the problem with no background. Listening intently will help you understand how the other person communicates and better be able to help solve their problems.

5. Keep a level head

There are many times during a consulting engagement where anxiety plays a role. I have on some occasions been frustrated and regretfully lost my cool. To develop credibility a consultant must keep a level head. One way to do this is to remember that this problem is theirs, and we are brought in to help solve it. We must work through the problem like it's our own but not internalize it and make it our own problem.

Also, interpersonal relationship issues can definitely cause problems. I was once with a client who had a manager who would quite often enter meetings and cause conflict. Most people would leave the room quite dejected, and you could often see the look in their eyes. It was as if they were thinking, *Here we go again.* Others would push back and get into arguments with him.

This was very difficult as it caused a lot of strain and often it took a long time for the dust to settle. As a consultant you must keep calm and be the voice of reason in a sometimes very confrontational and frustrating situation.

One way to stay calm is to decide ahead of time that you will remain level headed. Don't play scenarios in your head of you responding harshly to others, rather visualize scenarios where others are agitated or aggressive and you remain calm and stoic. Visualizing these scenarios will put you in a position to better respond calmly when situations arise.

6. Be objective

One major characteristic of credibility is objectiveness. When one is objective, others view that person to be more credible. This is sometimes difficult, especially when emotions are involved with decision making.

As consultants, you can increase objectivity by using the *7 Strategies for Making Objective Decisions* approach by Jayson Demers. The approach is to:

1. Acknowledge your biases
2. Develop a pro and con list
3. Document and tinker with assumptions
     a. Often we make decisions, and we have assumptions in our mind. Document those assumptions so that they are visible for everyone. This allows people to question the assumptions or be able to see where some decision-making is coming from.
     b. Tinkering with assumptions can also lead to credibility. In other words, you're asking, "If we alter our assumptions slightly, how does this affect our decisions?" Using this technique, you often gain credibility from participants because they realize you're not trying to push your own agenda.
4. Create a scoring system for decision making
5. Make the decision and live with it

We all draw on experience and have personal opinions and preferences however viewing solutions in an objective manner allows a consultant to provide the best recommendations to their clients. Be committed and diligent on your options and recommendations just as if your client's company was yours. However, make sure you use objectivity as an independent party to provide thoughtful non-emotional solutions.

7. Communicate effectively

Communicate often and in various forms. Email tends to be the most common form of communication, however email is often overused and loses its effect. Email will continue to be used during a project for the foreseeable future, but communicating in person, on the phone, or through meetings creates credibility and connection.

The communication should be authentic, professional, and of course, meaningful. I've seen many projects that have communication newsletters that serve little purpose to those who are reading it. The goal is not to communicate just to communicate. The goal is to communicate to open the lines of understanding between yourself as a consultant and those that you work with.

Also, avoid useless and unproductive meetings. Nothing can kill credibility for a consultant like facilitating an unproductive meeting that isn't required. Many clients' managers have standing weekly meetings that should be frequently cancelled. They go through this procedure with the idea that they are communicating effectively, or that something is better than nothing. This hurts the credibility of that manager. You need to be credible and reduce the needless and unproductive meetings. There are some great courses available to manage meetings effectively. Please check out a list of courses and bonus material available at https://theconsultingplaybook.com/bonus

8. Know what you know, and don't claim to know what you don't

It's important as a consultant to know what you know. It's not arrogant to state your opinion. Your clients are paying you for an opinion based on your knowledge, experience, and education. Most consultants don't have a problem with this, although some are on the humble side and occasionally underestimate or downplay the knowledge they have.

More often consultants will overestimate their knowledge. I had a long-term client that sold off their IT group to an international consulting company. The culture of the international company was to have their employees say they had strong skills in an area, if they were asked by someone, even if they did not have those skills. Then they would try to learn as much as they could as quickly as they could on that subject area. Sounds like staying one page ahead of the client, doesn't it?

Shortly after the purchase of my client the new company wanted to use internal resources for their projects which is very common and expected. At the time, I had more than 16 years of consulting experience and the firm brought in a resource to replace me. The resource coming in said that he was able to do a lot of work that they later found out he was not able to do. They found this out as he was to be placed on a project. As the project manager was asking very simple questions, the resource had relatively no answers, and the answers he did have were very vague or general. It wasn't long before the project manager became aware that the consulting resource didn't have the skills that were required to do the job. Soon, that new resource was let go from his employment, as he was not able to execute the work that both the company and the client were requiring.

To have credibility you should never downplay what you know, have experienced, or are able to do. However, you should never say you know things, are able to do something, or imply that you have experience that you don't. What I found in the course of my career is that most clients will have someone, be it an employee, consultant, or other resource working for them that knows more on a specific topic than many consultants. If a consultant is stretching the truth, there will likely be somebody in the organization that will eventually find that out.

You can also leverage the expertise of other consultants and experts when there is subject matter that you are unfamiliar with or is outside of your area of expertise. Having a strong network of consultants and other resources that you can draw upon helps your network, your client and yourself.

9. Develop competence

Competence is one of the main areas that people describe as a consultant being credible. One challenge to remaining competent is the rate of information and change. Buckminster Fuller defined the "Knowledge Doubling Curve." Before 1900, he measured that knowledge was doubling every 100 years. After World War II, he measured that knowledge was doubling every 25 years. Currently it is believed that knowledge is doubling every 12 months, and soon, the knowledge doubling curve rate will be every 12 hours.

This requires a consultant to constantly be investing in their skills. You should be reading and learning consistently. Constant learning reduces the need for a full upgrade of your skills. Set aside at least 30 minutes per day to read. Implement what you learn in small amounts. This will provide you the benefit of the skill right away, and you will begin to make it a habit.

10. Build specialization through general skills

Throughout my consulting career I have noticed a consistent approach by top-notch consultants. The first thing that the best consultants do is develop a very strong foundation of general skills and knowledge. This can be in accounting, engineering, or computer programming, while others develop skills in areas like communications.

Once these general skills are put into practice, they become ingrained, and the consultant can start to develop specialized skills. In almost every area of consulting, this is how specialists are developed. After developing those specialized skills, the consultant is often given opportunities to broaden their skills, thus developing general skills again. They repeat this process over and over again, never abandoning their general skills and using their specialized skills to springboard their careers forward.

11. Commit to competence

To develop competence, a consultant must commit to their career and learning. Author and personal development coach Brian Tracy recommends that people invest 3% of their future earnings in education. This means if you want to earn $200,000 next year, you should invest $6,000 in your education this year.

My recommendation is that you set out a quarterly education objective based on your career goals and opportunities that you see in the marketplace. Those objectives should drive out your education steps. The internet is flooded with courses, information programs, and books that can distract you, not just with your time and energy but also with your money. It's good to have various interests and want to develop new skills. However, the shotgun effect of just trying to learn as much as you can in random areas will not allow you to remain competent.

Develop an education program for yourself and execute what you have learned right away.

12. Build confidence

Confidence is an area that every top consultant has which builds trust with the client. Have you ever spent time with someone where it is obvious they are lacking confidence? The result is that you question their abilities, isn't it? I once worked with a man who was a low talker, which meant he spoke very quietly. You had to struggle to hear him. He was a very capable and competent resource, but he lost credibility with almost everyone he worked with because of it. Those of us who worked with him daily developed other forms of affinity with him, but to others, his quiet talking suggested that he was not confident so they would discount what he said.

The following are some items you can do to increase your confidence:

Action	Impact	Benefit
Stop the inner critic	The inner critic voice we hear often tells us we aren't good enough or there is something wrong with us	Notice this voice, recognize it, and then tell yourself to stop. Focus yourself on something good you have done, and your mind will be free to continue
Remove negative human influences	Negative influences make us question ourselves and our decisions	Eliminate the negativity and burden from others

Stop complaining	Complaining fuels others' control over us and minimizes our own abilities to control the things we can control	Focus on the things that we can control and not events that are out of our control
Improve nutrition	Poor nutrition reduces our energy levels and impacts how we see ourselves	Good nutrition makes you feel better, and when you feel better, your confidence increases
Reduce alcohol consumption	Alcohol is a depressant and has negative effects on us	Your thoughts are clearer, and you are not weighed down with the impact of alcohol
Remove other negative influences, such as TV, movies and news	Over-consumption of these gives us a negative impact on how we see the world around us	Our conscious and subconscious minds are free from stories of despair, worry, hate, and other negative emotions

Another area to develop confidence is to keep a journal of good things that have happened to you and your life. When you feel like your confidence may be shaken, go to that journal and review how blessed you are. I recommend reviewing the journal frequently to remind yourself of your blessings.

One thing that I have found that has worked tremendously for me over the years is to keep a gratitude journal. The gratitude journal is where I write down all of the things I'm grateful for. I recommend waking up in the morning and immediately saying something that you're grateful for. A gratitude journal allows me to write down past, current, and future people, events, and things that I'm grateful for.

What I found during this process is that when I went into the past and remembered events that I once deemed as negative, I now realize how that experience has served me and helped me become the person I am today.

Lastly, as a consultant you must look for opportunities to stretch yourself. Individuals can find themselves in a boring stage in life and in their career because they are not capitalizing on opportunities to put themselves in situations where they can grow. To grow we must stress and strain ourselves to try to improve and learn new things. Routines will actually affect our confidence because things become boring. Our confidence improves drastically when we enter consulting because we are put under strain and must learn things quickly. As time goes on, our job becomes more routine and, although many of us have confidence in the areas we have expertise in, we may not have confidence in areas where we are not as familiar. This can cause avoidance of those areas. Try something new, learn something new, and get back to the stage when we were new consultants, were developing new skills, and your confidence will grow dramatically.

13. Exercise enthusiasm

Human beings like to be around enthusiastic people. The definition of enthusiasm is intense and eager enjoyment, interest, or approval. Synonyms include eagerness, keenness, passion, energy, and spirit.

When others are around people who have enthusiasm, the energy level goes up. They want to be around the enthusiastic person again. I'm not suggesting being like former Microsoft CEO Steve Ballmer, running around on stage yelling and sweating (although that paid off huge dividends for himself and his teams at Microsoft.) The reason it paid off was because Ballmer was being authentic in his enthusiasm. Even years after retiring and purchasing the Los Angeles Clippers, he still is extremely enthusiastic at basketball games.

Enthusiasm involves being positive, energetic, attentive, and engaged in the topic of conversation. The "As If" principle works on developing enthusiasm as well as other characteristics. The "As If" principle is, if you want to develop a trait or characteristic act, as if you already have it. The best way to use the "As If" principle is to find others that have the traits you are looking for and model those traits.

Find someone who you deem to be enthusiastic and look at their actions. Their eyes will likely be enlarged, they will be smiling, they'll be sitting upright or even standing. When you find someone who's enthusiastic, imitate their body language. One way to become enthusiastic is to simply smile. Smiling will create energy within and around you that begins to generate positivity.

Tony Robbins talks about getting into state. This means getting into the physical state for the emotion or characteristic that you want to portray. Standing upright, shoulders back, chin up with a smile will put you in an enthusiastic state. Once you are in the physical state the emotion and characteristics will follow.

14. Gain and draw on experience
Credibility is also driven from experience. This doesn't mean longevity, as often people believe that because they have put their time in, they deserve the rewards. There is a saying that one person may have 20 years of experience, and another person has 1 year of experience 20 times. Longevity does not always mean experience.

In my previous book, *The Consultant's Code,* I talk about focused effort being one of the pillars of consulting success. Focused effort is required to gain experience. A consultant can reduce the amount of time to develop experience by focusing.

Learning from others, such as reading books and watching how other great consultants, managers, and other resources perform their work, also allows us to gain experience. This is why professional sports like the National Football League have their top rookie quarterbacks play the role of a back up their first and possibly second seasons. This allows them to not only learn the new system, but also witness how a veteran quarterback behaves.

Remember though that you can't just learn by watching. The NFL quarterback at some point needs to get off the sidelines and onto the field. You can't watch forever, so remember that the goal is to get in the game.

Experience can also be gained by volunteering and taking on new roles and opportunities. I've often seen consultants step up to do things that are outside of their area of expertise. This provides different opportunities to gain more knowledge and experience. Consultants that try to reduce their workload are not provided the same opportunities as those who are constantly looking for ways of developing their skills.

15. Modelling
Possibly one of the best ways to develop credibility is by modelling those that are successful. Modelling is using a proven approach to undertake an activity. Some people lose credibility because they are executing a model that does not work for the situation at hand. Some people make up an approach as they go and they hope for the best. Modelling allows us to follow someone who has already been successful. Modelling works best when you have a step by step guide to follow. This is why books provide so much value because the steps are defined. We can also model others by watching. Find someone who is successful and watch what they do. Better yet, ask them questions and find out firsthand.

Be careful in the models you select. If you select the wrong model you will get the wrong results. Ask yourself, is the person I am modelling living a life that I would like to live? Are all of their results something I would be proud of if it was me? Am I willing to make the same sacrifices? If the answers are Yes, then start modelling. If not, then select someone else. But always choose wisely.

16. Remember to social distance

The COVID-19 coronavirus pandemic made the term social distancing a part of our everyday language. However, we need to use social distancing from other threats including negative connections and damaging profiles on social media. Clients, employers and even other consultants will examine your online profiles on social media platforms. Even a simple internet search on your name could bring up negative information that could damage your credibility.

It is not uncommon to hear of someone being let go from a job or contract due to posts, responses or images that do not meet the minimum standards of the company you work for. Most companies require their consultants to sign Code of Conduct Agreements. If you violate the Code of Conduct your contract can be terminated.

In the year 2020 we witnessed countless videos of people behaving in offensive ways that caused them to lose tremendous amounts of credibility and trust. This resulted in those individuals losing their jobs, businesses and even affecting family members' employment. Posting negative statements, liking or sharing offensive opinions from others, or being included in pictures of hateful acts have all cost individuals' opportunities.

Although they seem like extreme examples this happens frequently. Clients will use social media searches to investigate the consultants they hire. Make sure that the people you are associated with and connected to online share your values and you are proud of them. Ensure the posts you create, like or share is information that your clients would also agree with. If you think there is a chance that the information may violate the beliefs of your client then don't link yourself to it or you must accept the negative consequences that may come from being associated with the information.

You can use social media in a constructive manner by associating yourself with positive information. It can also be used to share information related to your industry or area of expertise thus differentiating yourself from others. However, you must have a clear approach to how you use social media and be fully aware of the potential benefit when used wisely or negative consequences when used foolishly.

Use social media. Don't let social media use you.

17. Take advantage of mentorship and coaching
We can't learn everything on our own. Even one the greatest golfers of all-time, Tiger Woods, has a coach. The greatest actors use coaches to help them develop new skills and prepare for new roles. Mentors and advisors can help you avoid hazards in your career and

life. Almost all of the great businesspeople, consultants, athletes, and other professionals use mentors to help them.

Skills and direction that you can get from a coach and mentor can help you develop credibility. Having an answer in itself does not create credibility, although the outcomes of having a coach and mentor will help you avoid hazards and take advantage of opportunities, which will develop credibility. Choosing a coach or mentor takes humility and you have to be willing to be vulnerable and accept the advice that might really stretch your capabilities and attitude.

I was fortunate throughout my career to have more experienced consultants and other businesspeople act as mentors for me. They provided advice and guidance, which helped me not only feel connected but not feel alone and stranded.

I recommend finding a mentor or coach to help you. I also recommend mentoring others to develop your skills at helping others and seeing challenges, problems, and issues from a different angle.

If you need help finding a mentor or coach access additional information at https://theconsultingplaybook.com/bonus

Credibility and Three-Way Trust

Remember to develop credibility to strengthen your triangle and develop the three directions of trust; how the client trusts you, how you trust the client and how you trust yourself. By keeping this in mind you will strengthen your credibility and have a solid building block to becoming a trusted advisor.

Trust Exercise - Credibility

Use the information in this section to analyze where you and others develop trust through credibility. Also, you'll be able to review relationships where trust is lacking due to deficient credibility. Ask yourself if you are exercising personal responsibility when developing credibility.

By developing the ability to review relationships in this way you will be able to identify missing elements which add conflict and pressure to interactions. It will also allow you the ability to better recognize others that have skills that align with your goals and objectives which enable meaningful and rewarding relationships.

Taking the Next Step: Giving Back

As we conclude our discussions about each section, we will discuss giving back. This is because everything you do is not just for you. You must give back. The universe requires it. One of the things that motivated me to write my books is that I've been blessed throughout my life by many mentors who assisted me. Each one provided me something new and something special. I wanted to share what I've learned during my life and career with others because others provided that to me.

In this section, you've learned methods of building credibility, through mentorship, enthusiasm, gaining and using your experience, and focusing. These methods will make you a better consultant and person. I request that you share what you've learned with others. Please pass along any new methodologies or approaches you've learned or write articles on the information. There are three main results that occur from giving back to others in this way:

1. You become an expert

Credibility in its own right will cause you to be seen as an expert. By giving and sharing you will be seen as the go-to person by your clients, peers, and others. This makes you be in demand and a sought-after consultant.

2. You become a positive example

Being credible provides a positive example for those around you. We're not perfect, but the world needs more credible people. The universe will reward you because of your credibility as an example to others to achieve more.

3. You help yourself

Each time you use the skills related to credibility you develop the credibility muscles. You will be stronger in those areas, and it will be easier to apply those skills. This will make your life easier by giving back to others and teaching others skills. You must be credible before you can be incredible.

Section 2: Authenticity

Chapter 4: Authenticity and Trust

"Authenticity is the alignment of head, mouth, heart, and feet - thinking, saying, feeling, and doing the same thing - consistently. This builds trust, and followers love leaders they can trust." -Lance Secretan

In 1925, Bobby Jones, one of the greatest golfers of all time, called an infraction on himself in the first round of a tournament. The penalty for the infraction was a one stroke penalty. At the end of the tournament, he and another golfer were tied. This resulted in 35 playoff holes to determine the winner. For those that know very little about golf, one round of golf that takes a professional player more than 4 hours to play is 18 holes, and they usually play that in one day.

Jones ended up losing the playoff and the tournament. After the tournament, Jones was commended for being honest and calling the infraction on himself in the first round of the tournament. Had he not called that infraction, he would have won the tournament outright without requiring the playoff. Jones responded to the compliment with a statement: "You might as well praise a man for not robbing a bank."

To him being honest was just a fact and something that was innate in him. He saw no reason why someone should be recognized for being honest. This is a truly authentic human being.

What We Think Authenticity Is

Often people think that to become authentic you can just do whatever you feel and be whoever you want to be. This is definitely not the case. I once worked with a gentleman who had tattoos all over his body. This was in 1999, and tattoos were common, yet not as acceptable as they are today. He was a very clean-cut looking guy and would wear long-sleeve shirts up to his wrist, as his tattoos were all over his arms and down to his wrist. He did this out of being sincere and authentic, as the role as a consultant in large software implementations required him to have a certain look. Now one might say, "Is that really being authentic to himself? Shouldn't he just roll the sleeves up and show his tattoos if that's who he is?" The challenge with that type of thinking is that we play many roles in our lives, and we need to be authentic to the role that we are asked or required to play.

What Authenticity Actually Is

When we refer to someone as being authentic or sincere, we are really saying that they act genuine and they aren't hypocritical. Although being labelled as authentic or sincere is a compliment, you have to ask yourself if the opposite is that common?

It may or may not be common, however, we are inundated with stories of people that have been found out to be insincere and inauthentic. So, when we are able to determine that someone is authentic or acting with sincerity, our society glorifies that behavior.

As consultants we have exactly the same requirements upon us. There are times when we have to bring in a little bit of conflict to our client sites. There are times where we need to be the therapist for our clients. Other times we need to be the coach and give them a kick in the pants. And sometimes, we're the ones receiving a kick.

I once worked for a client where many of the employees were struggling to execute their work on time. The employees had plenty of time yet chose distractions and did not focus on the deadlines they were provided. As an external consultant, I went to the project manager, and I told her. "In this next meeting, if you need to punish somebody you can punish me. You can yell at me, threaten me, whatever you need to do to get the word across that missing these deadlines is not acceptable." I told her, "The only thing I request is that you tell me that ahead of time so that I'm aware that this is what is required in this meeting." Her eyes got very big, and I think she was taken back that I would make such an offer. My thought was to set the stage for everyone else to realize that if she's going to yell at me, she must not be very happy. That's an extreme example about being authentic to a role. I was willing to be the example to get the point across if that helped out the team.

Why Authenticity Is Important for Consultants

Authenticity is important for consultants because you are expected to play many roles in your life and career. If you are not authentic, then you will be hard pressed to determine where you end and the role you are expected to play begins. This can be a challenge for less experienced consultants who feel like they can't be themselves. It is important to be authentic, as clients are looking for people who can fit into their organization. When you are authentic, the client sees the real you even if you are still playing a role.

We Recognize Authenticity in Others

We usually have limited or no history when we go to work for a client. This can be challenging but also a blessing. It's important to remember that this client and their staff have existed long before we came along to help them. The reason for understanding this is that their staff may not be acting authentically as corporate culture, measurements and reviews, and disciplinary history have molded the organization and their employees.

What I have found over the years is that the corporate culture is derived by the founder's business ideology. I think of the business ideology as being the forms to a foundation of a building. The corporate culture is the concrete that is poured into the forms. Once the corporate culture solidifies, it becomes very difficult but not impossible to change. The longer that corporate culture has cured, the more difficult it is to change. As consultants we need to be aware of this.

What we often find as we work for clients over a long period of time is that the way their employees act on site and in the office is not who they really are. I've seen situations where employees who played the role of someone who just can't get an idea are actually extremely bright and creative as soon as they leave the office. Others cause conflict, distraction, and delay throughout the day, yet are the most helpful people when they leave work.

Now we can argue that this is the role they're supposed to play. I believe there are situations for people to play positive roles in an organization, but negative roles need to be weeded out. As consultants, if we're not brought in to reorganize their organization, then we must function with what we've been provided. However, when we get a glimpse of the authentic person, we're able to work with them better and actually manage them better. We can also find ways to encourage and support the authentic employee so they can achieve more in their career.

I once worked for a client where the manager of financial accounting didn't like to engage in any form of conflict with any of the staff. Malcolm was a very nice guy and did his job very well, but one of the roles of a manager of financial accounting is to deliver bad news or to be able to say "no" more times than you say "yes."

Malcolm hired Sandra as the supervisor of financial accounting and asked her to be the gatekeeper and put pressure on the departments that they supported. Sandra's role was to question and get justifications for every decision that was to come through their department.

The challenge with this was that Sandra was not suited for that role in a sense that her personality was one of collaboration and not of conflict. She preferred to work with others to achieve their objectives rather than be a gatekeeper of the checkbook. Over the course of her two years in that position, relationships were very strained between her and most of the staff. Being an external consultant, I was used to having or noticing these types of relationships, although the non-collaborative approach that she was encouraged to take on put up many obstacles for me and my team.

Fast forward two years later, and she was put in a much different role. This allowed her to collaborate with people and provide her expertise that she had rather than trying to control the purse strings of the organization.

Sandra ended up being a fantastic resource and continues to be one of the most valuable resources for this company to this day. I've had meetings with people in this organization who rely on her for her expertise. I've heard others personally requesting her to be involved with the work they are doing because she contributes so much to their teams.

The challenge Sandra faced was that she was not being authentic. She was asked to play a role of being confrontational rather than collaborative. Oddly enough, because she's in a more authentic role today, she actually feels the freedom to be able to speak her mind and play the devil's advocate. This is an area where someone was put in a position or asked to play a role where they were not authentic or felt that they could not be authentic to themselves.

Others Recognize Authenticity in Us

Many years ago, I heard of a list that then Dallas Cowboys Head Coach Bill Parcells provided to his quarterbacks including Tony Romo. One of the items on the list was that a quarterback cannot be a joker. He said that players will not follow a joker. I took this to heart, and for the next six months, I played out of my authentic self and tried to be a character that avoided humor or fun at all costs.

During this time I never felt authentic. I felt very awkward, like I was not being myself. Then one day I thought about the statement that caused me to change my behavior. I thought of the number of quarterbacks that did use humor on the field, including Joe Namath, Terry Bradshaw, and Brett Favre. I realize that they were able to use humor to get through tough times but still focus and execute.

One example is when the Green Bay Packers were going into an overtime game in the playoffs. In overtime, there is a coin toss to decide who will receive the ball. Each NFL team has six captains, and they attend the coin toss at center field. As Brett Farve and the other captains were walking to the center field, Farve said to one player on his team who was wearing a stocking hat, "Hey, did you hear what happened in Milwaukee last night?" The player looked at him and said, "No," and Farve quickly responded, "The lights went out!" He then quickly pulled the stocking hat over the player's eyes.

As silly as that was, he was able to use humor during a stressful moment going into overtime but was also able to focus and get back to work quickly. This was his authentic self.

After realizing that others use humor and are not all buttoned up all the time, I allowed humor to come back into my daily activity. I looked on the brighter side of things, smiled more, and try to find humor in many situations. This allowed me and the teams I work with to weather some very difficult situations.

We Recognize Authenticity in Ourselves

This is where we need to be true to ourselves. We do this by experiencing new things and questioning what we like and don't like. We live in a world where compassion and sincerity toward yourself is not encouraged. It may not be discouraged, but it's definitely not reinforced that being sincere toward yourself is a value worth building.

However, when people have terminal illnesses or when personal situations become very dire, human beings are encouraged by those around them to love themselves, be more compassionate toward themselves, and to do the things that they want to do. It shouldn't take a grave situation for human beings to find out and accept that being authentic, sincere, and compassionate toward ourselves is something worth building.

In fact, I believe many of the interpersonal issues we deal with are a result of one or both parties not being true to themselves. As we get older and we have less time on our score clock, we realize that being authentic to oneself might be one of the most important attributes a human being can have.

Throughout our life we must play different roles for ourselves. We are a provider when we are earning income, or a caregiver when we are taking care of ourselves, we are our own coach when we are encouraging and pushing ourselves to do more, and we're a friend when we need positive self-talk.

Each of these roles requires us to be authentic. It takes a lifetime to learn how to play these roles properly. As consultants, it's important to develop the roles required to support, be authentic, and sincere toward ourselves. The books that I write are meant to help share with you some of the lessons I've learned but each person has to develop their own authentic self.

Chapter 5: What the Experts Say About Authenticity

"Authenticity means erasing the gap between what you firmly believe inside and what you reveal to the outside world." -Adam Grant

There are various theories on authenticity. Authenticity has been an interest to researchers and individuals for a long time, however it has developed more interest in recent years.

The following are different concepts and theories regarding authenticity.

Trait Authenticity

Trait authenticity refers to authenticity as being a trait that someone has. There are various theories regarding trait authenticity, which include Self Determination Theory, Multicomponent Conceptualization and Person Centered.

1. Self Determination Theory

This theory was developed by Edward Deci and Richard Ryan in 1995. This theory is that individuals have three basic psychological needs which are:

- Autonomy
- Competence
- Relatedness

Autonomy is the power to make your own decisions without the interference from others. This is where you can make your own choices.

The ability to do something successfully, effectively and efficiently is competence. Competence is where you have the ability to do something.

Relatedness is where someone feels connected to others and has meaningful relationships. They feel part of a group, team or community.

When these basic psychological needs are met, then the person has the ability for authenticity. They suggested that autonomy and competence are especially important for developing authenticity as I believe both have an underlying value of personal responsibility.

I have found that consultants feel more freedom and act more authentic when they are capable and have competence. This is because they have confidence in their abilities to execute their work. They also often carry this into their personal lives. My experience is also that consultants that have freedom and are not restricted in performing their craft, which is autonomy, often are more authentic as they are not constrained by others through micromanaging or too much oversight.

When I chose to leave the consulting company I was working for in 2008 and start my own venture, I felt this way. There was fear but also a level of freedom that could not be felt previously. This also allowed me to be more authentic because I felt that I was allowed to be myself as I was ultimately responsible for my actions. This built strong relationships with clients and their employees resulting in more rewarding work.

2. Multicomponent Conceptualization of Authenticity

This theory was founded by Michael Kernis and Brian Goldman, and they defined authenticity as "the unobstructed operation of one's true or core self in one's daily enterprise." They further breakdown the theory into four components which are:

1. Awareness
   - being aware of one's emotions, strengths, desires, motivations, and weaknesses
2. Unbiased processing
   - the ability to objectively evaluate information that is relevant to one's self, regardless if the information is from internal or external sources
3. Behavior
   - this is acting in accordance to your values, needs, and preferences
4. Relational Orientation
   - the ability to share your true self with others in a close relationship

I want to point out that unbiased processing allows people to be authentic. Inauthentic individuals have a warped sense of self and are not able to take feedback or information and objectively use this to improve. As a consultant this is critical to be able to objectively evaluate this information as true or false.

Once I was on a conference call, and I heard an employee of the client say, "I don't think he is a good consultant." Right away someone said, "Your phone is not on mute." Now I can tell you this criticism hurt. After a few moments though, I thought, "I don't know who they are talking about." Because I was on the call I immediately assumed it was me, but I hadn't heard my name. I quickly thought, *Have I done a good job for them? Have I received compliments from those I worked with? Have they reached out to me to help them with many issues and challenges?* Each of those answers was yes. So I then thought, *I don't know who said this, and I don't know who he is talking about so I can't assume it is me.*

This is what unbiased processing allows. You can evaluate the information objectively about yourself.

3. Person Centered Model of Authenticity
This theory bases authenticity on three levels which are:
1. Primary Level
   - unconscious thoughts, emotions, and states of a person
2. Secondary Level
   - conscious thoughts, emotions, and states of a person
3. Third Level
   - lived experiences, behaviors, and expressed emotions

The first aspect of authenticity lives between levels 1 and 2. This is because our authentic selves are a reflection of our unconscious and conscious thoughts and emotions. The more those are in alignment, the more authentic someone will be.

For instance, if someone acts confident on a conscious level (level 2) but feels unconfident at the unconscious level (level 1), the person will act obnoxious, arrogant, and conceited. This is because their conscious and unconscious levels are misaligned.

The second aspect of the authenticity in regard to this theory is between level 2 and level 3. This is where the conscious levels of one's thoughts and emotions are in line with their experience and behavior.

For example, a consultant may be very aware of their level of integrity and honesty (level 2). However, if they act in a dishonest way (level 3), such as not providing all of the information available to a client which could result in a negative consequence to the client, the consultant would not feel authentic. This is because their actions are not aligned with their conscious emotions and values. If the person is aligned between level 2 and 3, this is called authentic living.

The last aspect is called Accepting External Influence. This is where a person uses external factors such as their friends, company, community, and other external influences to live authentically or to develop alienation.

In this example, we find consultants who may be working for an organization who feels inauthentic, but when they change organizations or clients, they feel they are more aligned with those around them, allowing for authentic living.

This feeling of being inauthentic for consultants will occur more often in the future. I notice that it is more common for individuals, including consultants, to want to align their efforts with an organization whose goals and purpose match their own personal objectives. They want to know they are making a difference and not just collecting a paycheck.

Indecisiveness

Another term for indecisiveness is decision difficulties. Indecisiveness affects all areas of trust, however it may be a debilitating problem when it comes to authenticity. This is because we keep questioning what we should be doing rather than making a decision and going with it. We question our decision-making ability and that affects how others trust us.

Indecision occurs when someone has difficulty making a decision in one specific area. In other words, they may have no problem making decisions in all other areas of their life but struggle to make a decision in one specific area.

Researchers Veerle Germeijs and Paul de Boeck
identified eleven descriptors of indecisiveness:

1. Deciding takes a long time
2. Deciding is perceived as difficult
3. Not knowing how to decide
4. Feeling uncertain during deciding
5. Delaying decisions
6. Avoiding decisions
7. Leaving decisions to others
8. Changing decisions
9. Worrying about decisions that have been made
10. Regretting decisions made
11. Calling oneself indecisive

Understanding these eleven descriptors helps us as
consultants as we can identify indecision in ourselves
and our clients. At times our clients need to make
difficult decisions and recognizing these traits can help
you help them.

In the Netherlands Journal of Psychology a document
named "A Psychology Theory of Indecision," Eric Rassin
writes that there are various factors that can contribute
to indecision. They can be:

- Perfectionism
- Intolerance of uncertainty
- Time pressure
- Importance of decision

Various behaviors are displayed when indecision occurs, which are broken into three categories in the table below:

Delay	Tunneling	Post-Decision
Procrastination	Narrowed Search	Worrying
Avoidance	Tunnel Vision	Checking
Information Search	Obsessive Focus	Decision Instability

When you notice this behavior in your clients or yourself, there may be indecision at work. The following chapter identifies steps to help deal with indecision and develop authentic behavior.

Chapter 6: How to Become More Authentic

"Truth is a point of view, but authenticity can't be faked."
-Peter Guber

This chapter will cover steps to developing authenticity. You will learn various ways of building on your authentic self.

Ron Wilmington's book, *Authenticity: The Head, Heart, and Soul of Selling,* describes a six-step process to create the most value for your clients. Those steps are:

1. Connect
This is where we build a connection, comfort, and rapport with your client.

2. Listen
This is where we listen to our client to understand their wants, needs, and requirements. Empathetic active listening is required.

3. Illustrate
Explain how you can meet your client's requirements.

4. Evaluate
Make sure your solutions are right for your client. If you or your solution is not the right fit, then you should find someone who can help your client.

5. Negotiate

Negotiation involves more than just negotiating and agreeing to contractual obligations. Negotiation also includes working through your client's concerns, feelings, and worries throughout the engagement.

6. Transact

This is where we deliver services to our client.

Wilmington explains the positive transformation to building this type of authenticity is:

1. Helping others in a positive manner releases endorphins in the brain, positively affecting your emotional and mental well-being.
2. Your clients trust you because of your sincere desire to help them, and they reciprocate those desires back to you.
3. A trust bond is created between you and your customers that develops a win-win relationship.

I saw a documentary when I was a teenager on people who required a certain amount of work weeks so they could get unemployment insurance benefits. They had these make-work projects, and they had a group of people that were to move rocks by hand from one pile about a hundred yards away and pile them up. The next week they returned to work, and they were to move the rocks back to where they originally were. Although the goal of this make-work project was to get the people enough work weeks so that they could collect unemployment insurance benefits, this was a demoralizing exercise. Perhaps those that designed it had that as part of the intent, however it is almost a form of cruelty. Those that took part in this project talked about how much it affected their psyche to do all that work and then have to do it again, moving the rocks back to where they came from.

Now logically one would think, *Why do you care? You're just putting the work in so that you can get the weeks completed so you can get unemployment insurance.* But this example shows that human beings have a built-in mechanism as part of our DNA to do something of value. It's part of our authentic self. Of course, those people went home at the end of the day and were happy they were getting the work to receive unemployment insurance benefits so they could survive. But they also felt horrible, used, and humiliated by being asked to do work that served no purpose.

To develop your authenticity you must know your purpose. This may be very difficult to know at a young age. As we get older, our authentic selves come out more easily as we may be less subject to constraints. When I don't shave for a few days, I don't look at others and think, *Man, they must think I'm a bum.* But I can tell you some people do. I once went to pick up some medication at the pharmacy, and I was wearing a ball cap and hadn't shaved for two or three days over a long weekend. The pharmacist was very rude to me and actually reduced the prescription amount that I was able to pick up, as it was obvious she did not trust me. I went to the pharmacy about a month later to pick up another prescription clean-shaven from work and in my business attire, and the same pharmacist treated me like I owned the place.

These scenarios occur, and I know that people make snap decisions based on how we look. Because of my age I did not take it badly because I knew the pharmacist had to make decisions on who was picking up medication for good reasons and who was picking up medication for nefarious reasons.

Of course, as consultants, being considered authentic and sincere puts us in a position where the client can begin to trust us. Unfortunately, over my decades of consulting experience, I have seen very few consultants execute authentically at the client site. Some of this is due to the stress of being under tight timelines, but it is also not knowing how to act while with our clients. Knowing your client and their needs and values will allow you to respond and interact with them more authentically.

Create Your Values

In *The Consultant's Code,* I discuss generating likeability through knowing your values. To be authentic a consultant must know their values. Without knowing your values, it is very difficult to have a baseline to measure yourself and to have a checkpoint.

1. Create your values
Your personal values help keep you out of trouble and identify what you should and shouldn't be doing. Think

of the biblical Ten Commandments for Christians. It's a list of things one should and shouldn't do. Your personal values identify the choices you will make before you are faced with a decision. For instance, if you value honesty, then when you're in a position to decide between honesty and dishonesty, your personal value will help direct you to the right choice. If you need to make a decision and you don't have a value identified, you'll need to decide on the spot, sometimes in mere moments.

I recommend creating a positive value list and a negative value list. The positive value list is the list of values that you want to develop and surround yourself with. The negative value list plays a different role. The negative value list is not meant to be the opposite of the positive value list. For instance, if you have honesty on your positive value list, then by definition dishonesty is not valued because it is the opposite. There is no need to list the opposite of your positive values.

The purpose of the negative value list is to identify the values, emotions and experiences that you would do anything to avoid or eliminate. You can go through your experiences that provided you the most discomfort. For instance, if you identify rejection, lack of control, failing and feeling helpless as negative values, then you are aware of the emotions that can trigger you to act unauthentically. Now watch for situations where these emotions arise or when you feel this way.

The following is an example of positive and negative values:

Positive Values	Negative Values
Honesty	Rejection
Love	Helplessness
Safety	Worthlessness
Generosity	Loss of Control

The purpose of this list is not to avoid situations where your negative values may appear, rather the purpose is to be able to plan for situations when they will arise so you are ready. Awareness and preparation are key to knowing what values you want to cultivate and which ones you need to restrain.

Please go to https://theconsultingplaybook.com/values to access information and instructions on developing your values and principles.

2. Live by your values

Now that you have your values, the real work begins. You need to live by your values. A consultant's goal should be to become a trusted advisor for your clients. You do this by living by your values. When you live by your values, your client knows what they will get. It doesn't always mean that they live by the same values, but when you set your boundaries by your values, your clients will know what they can expect from you.

Dealing with Indecisiveness

We all can become indecisive at times. However, chronic indecisiveness can be a problem and can affect a consultant and their ability to provide recommendations. Indecisiveness will affect our trust with ourselves as well.

To deal with indecisiveness you can do the following:

1. Trust your gut

We usually know the right thing to do right out of the gate. This is what we call a gut instinct. Indecision can come from knowing that our gut is telling us something different than our brain. This brain vs. gut debate that occurs within us can sometimes be caused by outside influences. Advertising, family, or friends may have their own idea of what you *"should"* be doing.

2. Meditate on the decision

Having meditation as part of your everyday routine will help with indecision. People of faith will talk about praying on a decision. If you hold a particular faith, then I would encourage you to pray when indecision strikes. Meditation also delivers the same type of result.

We'll often hear sayings like, "Get out of your own way," or "Get out of your head." These sayings mean that we are thinking too much and often in a state of fear. When we over think, we tend to develop scenarios that can cause anxiety.

Meditation and prayer will help alleviate those concerns and allow you to make a better decision then if you let your logical mind do the driving.

3. Use your crystal ball

Imagine in ten years how this decision will impact you. If you look out into the future and realize that this decision will have little impact on your quality of life, then it becomes easier to make a choice. However, decisions that seem to be almost irrelevant and fleeting can have a major impact on your life. If you look into the future and see that this apparently small decision has a major impact, then take your time. You may need to do an options and recommendations approach to yourself.

There are stories of immigrants throughout the early 1900s that would travel from Eastern European countries to Western coastal countries, like France, Italy, and Spain, to take a ship to start a new life. Often the migrants would step onto ships with no real idea of where the ship was headed. Some people would get on a ship headed for the United States or Canada, and others would board ships for South American countries. I often wonder if those boarding the ships could've had more information and used the crystal ball technique, would they have asked more questions. Was going to New York or Montreal the best decision? Or would others, knowing they were headed for a less developed country, have changed ships to come to North America? I can't answer that, but I find it an interesting thought.

4. Imagine your ideal state

Often, worry and indecision can cause us to have a view of a negative future. In fact, the negative view is what causes indecision. As those thoughts continue, our worry becomes worse, and the cycle of stress and worry continues.

To deal with this, identify your ideal state. Write down exactly what the ideal scenario would look like. If you have time, do this over the course of multiple days. This sets your mind to what you want and not what you fear, generating a clearer mind. You will also begin to manifest what it is that you want. You'll begin to feel like a child looking forward to your birthday or other large event where you will receive something fun.

Also, if your decision requires an approval or negotiation from another party, then you are in the proper frame of mind to work with another individual on a solution. Those who are in fear act and react in ways that cause conflict, sabotage, or another negative behavior. Imagining your ideal state will put you in a mindset that shows you that your goals and wants are achievable.

5. Not deciding is deciding

By not deciding, you are actually deciding to let time (and likely someone else) make a decision for you. This is not where you want to be. I'm not suggesting that someone should go out and make any rash decision that comes to their mind. We should all do our due diligence when we make a decision. However, a lack of decision can paralyze us.

I realized early in my career that I didn't want to let others decide for me how my career would operate. This didn't mean that I didn't look for input or suggestions from others; however, I was making the conscious choice to be responsible for my career. This decision required me to take ownership of the choices that worked out and were successful but also those choices which ended with undesirable results.

6. Seek guidance

Guidance from others is a very useful approach when you run into indecision. Often others have either experienced the same type of challenge or are objective enough to ask questions and help guide you through the concern.

When seeking guidance, you should find someone that you trust and not share your concerns with others that could take on your stress. Often family members have your goodwill in mind and will take on your stress, and that can cause the situation to become even more stressful. My recommendation is to develop relationships with those that you view as a mentor or coach. Developing these relationships before you need help builds a rapport that allows the other party to know you and your situation better.

7. Practice on small decisions

If you find there are areas of your life where you find it very difficult to make a decision or you feel overwhelmed, you can work on making decisions with small things. Try a new dish at your favorite restaurant. Drive a new direction to work or alter up your routine a bit. These types of small decisions will build, and you will develop more confidence in making larger decisions.

Additional Ways to Become More Authentic

1. Do a self-check

Not only should consultants do self-checks, but each person should frequently perform a self-check. What this means is you should take time to evaluate how you have been acting and conducting yourself. Compare yourself to your values and ask yourself if you have been following your values.

Also, you can perform a self-check by simply asking yourself how you feel. Stress can be caused through guilt. If you feel guilty, ask yourself what you may have done, or experienced, or participated in that could have caused you to feel guilt. There are times where we feel guilty for something that is very minor.

I remember feeling guilty once and the guilt seemed to almost come from nowhere, which is not uncommon. After I did a self-check, I realized that my guilt was driven from walking away from someone during a conversation. It may seem odd to walk away from someone while you're talking with them however, I've noticed that when someone is deep in their thoughts they can be oblivious to those around them, even if those thoughts arise during a conversation.

I once had someone who apologized to me because she felt guilty for ignoring me in the hallway after she had received bad news on another matter. As she walked by me, I said hello, and she just looked at me with an angry look on her face. The next day she contacted me and apologized.

We also feel guilty for things that we do that are more major. It could be snapping at a client or doing subpar work. When you do a self-check, ask yourself what things could be causing you to feel guilty and begin writing them down. You may find that there are layers of guilt or stress piled on each other.

Guilt is an important indicator. It tells us that we may have done something that violated our values or we harmed someone or something that we care about.

The purpose of this is to try to make the situation right. If you found you hurt someone or did something outside of your authentic self then try to correct it. Once corrected forgive yourself and move on. Holding onto guilt is a form of self-punishment and it will be very difficult to be authentic while you are self-loathing.

We're all human beings, and we all make mistakes. But to continue with your authentic self, you must be able to do self-checks regularly to correct any behavior. As adults we are expected to parent ourselves and must put in steps to do so.

2. Meditate daily

As stated earlier, meditation serves many purposes, and one is to help us find our true selves. We live in a very busy time, and we have to build in a checkpoint to be able to clear our minds from the hectic noisy world we live in. We don't need to wait for indecision to start meditating. Meditating can help deal with indecision before it strikes. Meditation opens up many opportunities for people to find their authentic selves.

Don't get stressed by this idea. It can be as simple as just letting your mind not think of anything stressful or not focusing on priorities for thirty seconds. You can focus on your breathing before you start your day or begin something challenging. Meditation also helps put things in perspective and reminds us that many of the events that stress us out are not as daunting as we often think.

3. Don't be perfect

Oddly enough, people view others as authentic when they aren't perfect. In fact, we will often hear people say, "I don't trust that person; he's just too perfect." People must realize that even consultants are not perfect.

This doesn't mean to go out and purposely make mistakes to show you're not perfect. Life has a way of making sure that you make mistakes, even when you're trying to perform effectively. What this means is to show your vulnerability to others. You can share thoughts like, *I'm concerned,* or *I'm worried,* and be open to showing that you're not perfect.

Often consultants have the idea that they must be seen as a perfect, stoic, immovable, unemotional object. This is not the case. Clients want to connect with people who seem like everyday, normal human beings. It doesn't mean that you should air all your dirty laundry or show every imperfection that you are hiding. But it does mean that you are not required to cover up every blemish or be ashamed of who you are.

Clients have said it's a breath of fresh air to find a consultant who is authentic and personable and is not always trying to be perfect.

4. Develop strong connections

Some of my best friends and strongest relationships came from projects I worked on. I'm fortunate to have friends all over North America as well as some in Europe and Asia that I worked with over the course of my career.

I also have very strong connections with people that I grew up with as well as other people I became friends with as an adult. These connections help ground me and remind me who I am. This continues to help me develop my authentic self.

What we find with friends is that our friends say as much about us as they do about themselves. When somebody has strong, close, responsible and respectful friends, that usually says that they themselves are responsible and respectful. We still make mistakes and do things that are outside of our behavior, however strong connections solidify our authentic personalities.

Remember, it isn't a competition. You don't need to have lots of friends. Having a few close friends is more valuable than lots of acquaintances.

5. Be client-focused

Often, consultants are focused on their own needs, and they do this by being transactionally focused. Being transactionally focused means that the consultant is concerned about completing the transaction and delivering the service only based on what has been agreed to with the client. It also means that the consultant is focused only on the present rather than balancing it with future opportunities.

There are also situations where a consultant is survival focused. In these situations the consultant is only worried about finding their next job and billing as many hours as possible to take care of their own survival. If you're an independent consultant, there are likely times in your career where you may be in this type of situation.

Concentrate on having the client's interests in mind. In the long run this will give you the highest income and also more referrals and longer contracts. Being client focused definitely develops trust with the client, as they can clearly see that the consultant's interest is focused on their needs.

6. Go home

I recently started to connect with some people through Facebook that I had grown up with. I grew up in a very small town named Vita which is in southern Manitoba in Canada.

As I started to connect and talk with some of them, it was like we didn't have decades between speaking. This has done something to me emotionally as I felt connected to where I feel that I'm from. Although most of us move around and are quite migratory, we all have a feeling like we're from somewhere. That somewhere for me is Vita. Oddly enough if I was to tell someone where I was from, I would actually tell them the name of the town where my parents currently live. But in my soul and in my heart, I'm from Vita.

That adds to my identity. I'm still myself with my own experiences, but those are the people that I grew up with. They are what help make me my authentic self. Bits of me make them authentic in the same way.

7. Be aware and present

One area that is becoming more and more difficult today with the amount of distractions that we face is being aware and present in the moment. People can lose authenticity when they are constantly looking at their phones or other technology, causing them to not be present with their clients.

Additionally, this trains our brains to constantly look for something of distraction. As people are talking we may notice them looking away, looking over their shoulder, or looking out the door in anticipation of something to distract them, even just for a moment. I'm guilty of this too but it's something that we all need to work on, especially today when the amount of stimulation that is available to us has been increasing rapidly.

One suggestion is to leave your phone at your desk when you're in a meeting. If you bring your laptop to a meeting to take notes, make sure that you're not lured into responding to email or working on other tasks. We may feel like we are not being productive when a meeting becomes boring or we're not involved in the immediate conversation. The challenge with this is that meetings must run their course, and too often, we must repeat information because people are distracted.

I worked with a previous client that had employees that would routinely bring their laptops to meetings to take notes. What they were really doing was working on other initiatives during the meeting. It was not uncommon to have to repeat what was said because the person who needed to respond was busy working on some other tasks not related to the meeting. I could say it became a widespread problem, as often I would look around and see five or six people heads down focused on other work.

Make sure as a consultant that you are not doing this. There are skills to efficiently run meetings. If you are in meetings that are inefficient, then develop the skills required to properly manage those meetings rather than taking the time to do other work.

Please visit https://theconsultingplaybook.com/bonus for more information on better managing meetings.

Authenticity and Three-Way Trust

Developing authenticity is a key component to enriching the three directions of trust; how the client trusts you, how you trust the client and how you trust yourself. Nurturing your authenticity is the second component to strengthening the triangle to becoming a trusted advisor.

Trust Exercise – Authenticity

The information in this section will help you identify where you and others develop trust through authenticity. You will also be able to review situations where authenticity is insufficient and straining the relationship.

By developing the ability to review relationships in this way you will be able to identify missing elements which add conflict and pressure to interactions. It will also allow you the ability to better recognize others that have skills that align with your goals and objectives which enable meaningful and rewarding relationships.

This also helps you discover who you are. Many people spend much of their lives trying to discoverer who they really are. Take responsibly to apply these skills to help with that journey.

Taking the Next Step: Giving Back

In this chapter, you've learned methods of building authenticity through being vulnerable, being connected, and reconnecting to your roots. I request that you share what you've learned with others. Please pass along any new methodologies or approaches you've learned or write articles on the information. There are three main results that occur from giving back to others in this way:

1. You become more identifiable and relatable

Authenticity is like a breath of fresh air for people. Your clients, peers, friends, and family will recognize you as more relatable and refreshing. This will increase the quality of your relationships.

2. You have the "je ne sais quoi"

This translates to English as, "I don't know what." It means an indefinable quality that makes someone distinctive or attractive. When you share authenticity with others, you are that distinctive, attractive person. People may not know why, but they will recognize something different in you than others. You will receive great benefits from being distinctive.

3. You allow yourself to be yourself

When you share the skills that you have learned about being authentic, you solidify the qualities that make you, you. You are reinforcing those skills and allowing yourself permission to be you. This is where true freedom can be felt.

Section 3: Reliability

Chapter 7: Reliability and Trust

"The most successful people I know are also the most reliable." -Wayne Gerard Trotman

After the birth of my son in 2004, the client I was working for allowed me to work from home. I was very fortunate, however this did bring with it other types of challenges. Very often I would take phone calls throughout the evening while I should've been spending time with my wife and newborn. Eventually I had to become more reliable to myself and my family by telling the client that I would not take phone calls after a certain time. This was a difficult conversation as I did not want to appear to be unreliable, especially after setting the expectation that the client could call me any time while I was at home.

This is a balancing act that every consultant needs to go through, but reliability, like all four components of trust, goes three ways: We must be reliable to our clients, our clients must be reliable to us, and we must all be reliable to ourselves.

What We Think Reliability Is

Is reliability being on time? Or being where you are expected to be? Punctuality is an important skill, but is it the whole story? Others believe reliability to mean being accessible all of the time. That's definitely what I first thought when my son was born.

Consulting is a demanding career. Clients, employers, family, and other demands can cause us to feel like we are being pulled in many directions. Being there when others *always* need, and, in some cases, just want us to be can be a difficult and almost unachievable goal.

What Reliability Actually Is

Reliability is the quality of being trustworthy or of performing consistently well. This is different from simply being on time because it's measured over a long period.

Reliability can also be negative in the sense that someone might say that airlines are reliably late. We often know people who are always reliably late. We call this the devil you know vs. the devil you don't know. Often consultants may complain about their client and some of their deficiencies. However, when they go to a new client, they realize that the old client's deficiencies were at least known, so they could plan for them, while the new client's deficiencies still needed to be learned.

Reliability is knowing that winter is coming, and spring follows winter, and summer follows spring, and autumn follows summer. Some people may not like winter; some people may not like spring. But knowing they're coming allows us to prepare. Some people love spontaneity, but human beings in general prefer reliability—especially when it comes to their consultants.

Why Reliability Is Important for Consultants

Reliability is important for consultants, as our clients are depending on us to perform and behave in a consistent manner. This doesn't mean that sometimes we won't deviate from our consistent routine. But it does mean that trust is based on the fact that people can rely on us.

This is important for consultants as undoubtedly we're going to run into situations where we cannot achieve what we promised due to many external circumstances. How we deal with that changes depending on if the client still relies on us or if they believe we are not trustworthy. To sum this up: Making a mistake is not a big deal but owning up to it is. People do not want to see someone make the same mistakes multiple times.

I recall a client that had a project manager who was very unpredictable. This caused a lack of trust, as you would never know what mood this project manager would be in when you encountered her. This caused people to withhold information, avoid her, or ask others what mood she was in.

This is one example of a person who was not reliable and that lack of reliability caused a lack of trust.

We Recognize Reliability in Others

This story seems so far-fetched, maybe even almost unbelievable. Once I was working for a client in Toronto with four other consultants. One was local, and the rest of us were from other cities. The client was in telecommunications and was growing at a breakneck speed. We met the entire client team during our first meeting when we arrived.

After some introductions, the Director of IT, Harold, said, "Okay, you guys can now begin." When I started to ask some questions around their requirements, Harold stopped me and said, "We need two weeks' notice on any questions you'll ask before you can ask them."

I found this to be a very rare and very odd request to have to wait two weeks to get answers for questions that we needed promptly. Also, it would be very difficult to predict what questions I'd need answers for in two weeks, as the nature of projects evolved as questions and issues arose.

Fortunately, we ended up getting one on one time with many of their users and abandoned this two-week waiting period for answers. However, the oddities didn't stop there. The client demanded that the consultants be on site from 8 a.m. Monday morning to 5 p.m. Friday night. This is very difficult for three consultants who had to travel anywhere from two-hour to five-hour flights crossing multiple time zones. This would give most of us anywhere from a day and a half to only one day at home each weekend throughout the course of the project. Now on short projects that had a duration of a couple of weeks or maybe a month, this might be an acceptable approach. However, my experience is that consultants need to have a reasonable work-life balance and be able to go home to see their families.

We compromised as consultants and decided that we would stagger and overlap our schedules to make sure that there was coverage by one of us five days a week. This allowed the gentleman with a five-hour flight to be able to get home. Since my flight was only two hours, I would fly in on Sunday nights to be on site first thing Monday morning.

The next oddity came up when the client requested that all four of us work in one cubicle as they did not have enough space for all of their staff. The lack of meeting rooms prevented us from setting up in a meeting room and working there. Four people in a cubicle is not an acceptable way to work, so we tried to stagger our meetings and work from the coffee shop in the lobby. This took a lot of coordination between all of us to make sure that we had space to work as well as access to the IT system we were building. This was also prior to Wi-Fi and reliable virtual access so remote work was difficult.

The next strange event was that there were not enough chairs for everyone. So, we would have to get to the office very early in the morning to make sure we had a place to sit. We would often hear someone come in and say, "Oh no! I don't have a chair!"

Although I eventually came to enjoy working for this client, the odd behavior of the organization caused a lack of reliability and consistency in what we expected as consultants and just in basic employment working conditions. The result of being reliably disorganized was that we spent a tremendous amount of time and energy trying to achieve a goal that was already difficult and challenging without having distractions. This affected our trust with the organization and many of their managers.

Others Recognize Reliability in Us

When consultants are starting a new project, they frequently will be very amiable and agreeable. Then, once on site, a consultant may begin to renegotiate the terms of agreement. For many consultants, Monday to Thursday is a normal work week when travel is required. One consultant named Hugh changed up his working schedule and began working Tuesday to Friday, as he said this was a better schedule for him. The client agreed hesitantly to this change. A few weeks later, he didn't come in on a Tuesday, and instead, he showed up on Wednesday to say he'd now be working Wednesday to Saturday.

Work schedules on large consulting projects may not be as transparent and obvious as one might think. Many consultants report to managers who are not on site and have little interaction with the consultant. Project managers who are on site are responsible for the consultants who are at the client location. However, miscommunication, large project teams, and varying schedules can cause project managers to not always be aware of who is on site at all times. To sum it up: Everyone expects consultants to act like adults.

Because Hugh had changed his schedule on his own, the client and both the project manager and Hugh's reporting manager eventually lost trust in what he was doing. This resulted in Hugh being terminated, as the erratic and unreliable behavior was not consistent with what the client was expecting.

The two examples explained in this chapter may seem extreme however, it is not uncommon for consultants to start taking liberties with their clients as soon as they become comfortable with them. This is a big danger, as the client's expectations have been set, and we must continue to be as reliable throughout the engagement.

One area of reliability that has sprung up over the last number of years is remote working. Many clients are hesitant in allowing consultants to work remotely. They feel that if they can't see the consultant, then they don't know what they're doing. This is a challenge, as in reality, we are given components of work to do and are required to get them completed within the time expected. However, most businesses have not deviated from the industrial-age approach to managing people where they want to always see what they are doing. Sometimes a simple fix to potential erosion of trust is to offer more frequent status updates to the client. This way they can have more communication and concrete tracking of performance and results.

We Recognize Reliability in Ourselves

I worked with a gentleman named William who was once a consultant but is now an employee for one of my clients. He would come to work very early around 5:00 am. He would routinely leave the office long after everyone else was already home. He also would work weekends or on his days off if anyone in the company needed help.

He could operate at this pace for a few months until what would undoubtedly happen: He would get sick. It was not rare for an illness to cause him to be away from work for a week or even more. After recovering he would come back to work and repeat the process.

One might say that he was being very reliable to the company as he was always available. However, he was not being reliable to himself. If I worded it differently, he was stealing time from himself to give it to his employer. If he stole time from the company to do his own activities, he would likely get fired. My recommendation to anyone who is working these types of hours is to start to take more time for yourself. You need to be reliable to your needs. As consultants, although there will be times when your work feels like a sprint, it can be critical to ensure that you can pace yourself, more like a marathon, in order to sustain a career as a consultant and preserve and protect your health.

Chapter 8: What the Experts Say About Reliability

"Creativity isn't worth a thing if it isn't served with an equal amount of reliability." -Anton Peck

The definition of system reliability is "the probability that a system will perform satisfactorily for at least a given period of time under stated conditions of use." Human beings are not machines, but we are still measured on performing our activities in a predictable and acceptable manner.

As consultants we do not want to be measured as unreliable. To remove the emotion from the statement, we could state that an unreliable person is reliably inconsistent or consistently unreliable.

In the book *Credibility,* Kouzes and Posner state that "being open is especially important when discussing conduct that might look to others as inconsistent or incompatible with a prior promise. To enhance the reputation of being reliable you need to deal honestly with problems before they happen. As long as the problem is not recurring, you build confidence about your trustworthiness by demonstrating your initiative and by reassuring the other party that you care about the situation and are doing something about it."

One way to do this is properly map out the timelines for a project plan. Some activities are rushed or we don't plan any contingency time in case something happens. We should also plan out downtime for ourselves especially with longer engagements and projects because things will happen such as illness, conflicting requirements on our time or other unknown facts.

I had planned out a project for a client in Saskatchewan. The project was to go through the winter months and I estimated there to be about twelve weeks of work. When I presented the project plan I explained that there would be twelve weeks of effort spread across fourteen weeks of duration. The client was confused with why I would spread the work over an extra two weeks. I explained, the one thing I know about Saskatchewan is that there will be a blizzard that will negatively affect air travel. That will affect at least one week of the project. Also, undoubtedly some other known but unpredictable event, also called a known-unknown, will occur such as someone getting sick, unplanned absences, or other factors will occur and impact our timeline.

We have to plan these events into our timelines as they will occur. We also have to educate our clients that these events will happen and explain that we are prepared for them.

Types of Reliability

In psychology there are three methods of measuring reliability. These types of reliability are important to understand as consultants. This is because we can gain or lose trust based on these three types of reliability. Although these are based on research, these three types of reliability are common during consulting engagements.

Inter-rater Reliability (Across Different Individuals)

This type of reliability measures the consistency of the same test conducted by different people. In consulting this often happens when we ask a client how important something is. One person may say it's not very important, yet another says it's very important. It's critical as a consultant to work out any inconsistencies with our clients, and this form of reliability can do this.

From our client's perspective they also test consultants through this form of reliability. They do this by asking multiple consultants to grade particular types of work. For instance, a client may ask one consultant in a meeting "how difficult a particular task may be", and later ask a different consultant "is this task very difficult?" Asking two different people, the consultants, similar questions should have a consistent response. However, we know this doesn't always occur and can negatively affect the reliability of the information and the consultants. Understand that in consulting this will happen. Stay calm and ask questions to validate the information so you can provide the correct advice.

Test-Retest Reliability (Over Time)

This type of reliability measures the consistency of the same test being done over time. An example of this form of reliability giving someone the same test at two different times, it should result in the same or similar outcome. When we are dealing with our clients, we need to be aware of the answers we are receiving. When we ask the same question or similar questions to the same person, we should receive the same answer even when the question is asked at different times. However, in my consulting career I have seen numerous occasions where the same question resulted in different answers.

At one client I was to lead some testing. I had four users that were employees of the client that I was to coordinate and manage the test plan for. I asked one of the testers, named Wanda, if she had run through all of the test scenarios and if the results were as expected. She told me yes and that everything was fine and she would provide me with the test results. In a meeting the following day, I brought up the fact that Wanda had successfully completed her testing. Wanda followed up with, "No, I have a few more scenarios to run through." This is not the type of answer I wanted to receive after going on the record stating that Wanda had completed her testing. Things like this do occur, and this is why clients, project managers, and sponsors often confirm and re-confirm if particular work has been completed.

As consultants we are often asked the same question or a similar question by our clients. Sometimes our clients are testing us, other times they don't remember our answer, and other times they may have come up with a slightly different scenario.

The client will often use the original question as a baseline and expect the same answer. Make sure that you acknowledge that you have answered it previously, even if the context may have been different.

Internal-Consistency Reliability (Across Items)
This test measures the consistency of the individual items of a test. Internal-consistency reliability is based on testing similar items (across items) which should return a similar answer or result. For instance, if you were to ask if a basketball player could slam dunk and the answer was yes, and then you asked if the player can jump high and the answer was no, you would require more investigation. The two answers conflict so qualifying the questions and answers would be required.

An example of this would be satisfaction survey. You may ask someone if they are satisfied with the service and if they would recommend the service to someone else. You would assume that if the person answered yes to the satisfaction question, then they would say yes to also recommending the service to another person. If they answered no to the satisfaction question, and then answered yes that they would recommend the service, you would wonder why the answers are inconsistent. There may be valid reasons however someone not being satisfied with a service but would recommend the service would require some more investigation and analysis.

In consulting we sometimes see these types of results during change management. You may be in a meeting where a client says that they are interested in efficiency yet makes decisions or approves a business process that is less efficient. Often there are conflicting goals or unspoken criteria that causes these types of questionable decisions.

Clients may not have a scientific approach to evaluating inconsistencies however they are constantly monitoring the reliability of their consultants. Watch for inconsistencies when working with your clients as well. You can often catch challenges before they happen by noticing where expectations and behaviors conflict.

Uncertainty, Risk and Reliability

On February 12, 2002 Secretary of Defense Donald Rumsfeld used the term "known unknowns" when making the case for the American invasion of Iraq. When Rumsfeld used this term, he introduced this concept of trying to measure certainty to the general public. Although this term had not been previously used in everyday language this approach has been practiced in project risk management for many years prior to Mr. Rumsfeld making it popular.

Project Management Institute describes project risk as "the cumulative effect of the chances of uncertain occurrences adversely affecting project objectives." As consultants we need to be aware of uncertain events that can occur that may affect our reliability with our clients and ourselves.

There are four types of risk uncertainties that affect reliability. They are:

1. Known-Knowns
   - things or events we are certain of
2. Known-Unknowns
   - things or events we are aware of but cannot predict
3. Unknown-Knowns
   - things or events that others are aware of but we are not
4. Unknown-Unknowns
   - things or events that we are unable to know

Known-Knowns
These are events that we are aware of and can properly plan for. In fact, known-knowns provide no uncertainty because we are aware of them. For example, if you have vacation planned for two weeks in November then you need to communicate that to your client to set their expectations. Unfortunately, too many consultants negatively impact their reliability by not sharing known-knowns with their clients to properly set expectations.

Known-Unknowns
Known-unknowns are events that we are aware of but can not predict. Remember my story about the project plan in Saskatchewan. This is an example of a known-unknown. We know there will be a snowstorm in Saskatchewan, we just don't know when, where and how

severe it will be. Therefore, we need a contingency plan for the known-unknowns.

Unknown-Knowns

This form of uncertainty is based on the concept that as consultants we don't have all the information of what is happening or what may happen. However, others may have information about the event that is unknown to us. I know some financial investors who will always enter a deal assuming that the other person they are negotiating with has information that the investor does not.

Unknown-Unknowns

This form of uncertainty is based on the fact that we have no information available or we don't have the ability to gather the information. When someone uses the phrase "We don't know what we don't know" they are referring to unknown-unknown uncertainty. This is when an event seems to happen with no warning or without reason.

The four types of risk uncertainties can help with every day decisions and should be part of your decision making tool box. Categorizing information under one of these uncertainties can help you make better decision, focus on tasks that you can control and better plan for unknown scenarios.

Chapter 9: How to Become More Reliable

"It has always been my contention that an individual who can be relied upon to be himself and to be honest unto himself can be relied upon in every other way." -J Paul Getty

I once had another consultant ask me how he would be able to work from home, as I was given the privilege by the same client to work remotely. My response to him was, "You need to be able to show that you can work when you are on site in their office." What I noticed from this consultant was that he would routinely come in late and would often leave at the same time the employees would leave. I would tell him that he needed to be there in the office before others get in. He didn't need to be the first one in, but he couldn't be the last one. He also didn't need to stay until 9 p.m., but he could not be the first one leaving at 5 p.m.

The client allowed this consultant to work from home for a few weeks. Unfortunately, what happened was that he missed conference calls. There was a time zone difference between where he lived and the location of the client. Sometimes he would get confused about what time the conference call was. This is part of losing trust, and the client finally came to the conclusion that he was unreliable. You can guess what happened next. The client told him he was not allowed to work from home any longer.

What I did with that same client (even though I had worked for years remotely) is send a routine email to them so they knew my schedule. If I was going to get my son from school or even go out for lunch, I would email them and let them know that I would be away for an hour, or fifteen minutes, or whatever length of time I thought it would be. This told them that if they sent me an email, I was not going to be responding in that certain amount of time. I would always offer that if they needed to reach me right away, then they could always phone my cell phone.

This small step of just informing the client of where I was let them feel like they could rely on me as they knew where I was going to be.

Dealing with the Three Types of Reliability

In the previous chapter we talked about the three types of reliability and how we experience each during our consulting engagements. Following are ways to be able to deal with these types of reliability.

Dealing with Inter-rater Reliability (Across Different Individuals)

This is where we ask people to score, measure, or categorize something expecting the same type of measurement by different individuals. Often as consultants if we were to ask our clients a question that requires a subjective response, we may receive different types of answers from different people. One person at the client site might say that something is very difficult, while someone else might say it is low in difficulty.

This might seem like a problem; however, as consultants, we should always be looking for contradictions when engaging with our clients. The reason for this is that we need to flesh out any misconceptions or contradictions that are occurring with our clients and their businesses. The easiest way to do that is for us to take our objectivity and lack of in-depth knowledge to our client to ask questions.

When we find inconsistencies, we need to dig deeper. If two people measure something differently, we should immediately start asking questions. We can ask them to explain the process to get an idea of how difficult something is. We often sigh in relief when we hear that a client measures something to be simple or easy. However, we should pay just as much attention when someone says something is simple and still ask a few questions to make sure it is as simple as they say. Any parent with a school aged child will know that children often say, "I didn't get much homework, and the homework that I did get was really easy to do." Of course, we find out later that they have a big project that's due in a day or two that will take many hours to complete. As a consultant these types of scenarios can also occur. However, we need to get a real grip about what our clients are saying and how they are measuring or categorizing subjective questions.

When it comes to our clients testing us in regard to providing estimates, such as how difficult a solution is or how long it may take to implement, two consultants may give two different responses. This will lose trust, especially if the client feels that there is now a commitment with a lower estimate. Every consulting firm has been burned because a consultant has gone out on a limb and pulled an estimate out of the air, but the client felt that it was a commitment to complete that task in the time frame given. You can deal with this type of scenario by deciding ahead of time which consultant has the authority to make a decision of that magnitude.

There should never be a concern about asking for more time to do more evaluations. If you feel pressured to make a decision on the spot give yourself more time. The urgency close is one of the most effective ways to close a sale which is why it is used so often. In the urgency close the salesperson uses scarcity to their advantage. They may say something like "Limited time offer," or, "Offer ends at midnight tonight." Clients use the urgency close in different ways. They may say something like, "We have all the decision makers in the room right now, so let us know what it will take so we can decide right here." Don't fall for this tactic. If you don't feel comfortable giving an estimate, stand by your ground and tell them you need some more time. It is better to take additional time and get the right answer then be held by an arbitrary decision.

When we are dealing with ourselves this is a common trap. As consultants we may be our own manager and we're also the resource doing the work. This is especially true for independent consultants, but I stress that all consultants need to manage themselves effectively.

It is common for consultants to overpromise and underdeliver. This is not by choice, rather they are trying to make the client happy, or they haven't learned to say no properly. Other times they are choosing to ignore other commitments and hope that all of their obligations can be met. In some cases, their over-enthusiasm for the contract might cause them to promise or agree to timelines that can't adequately be achieved.

I present another way to deal with this. If you changed roles and you were playing the role of a manager, would you commit another person to delivering a result without talking to them and planning it out first? If you did this frequently that person may not work for you very long or you would at least have some conflict on your hands.

This is exactly what happens to many consultants. They end up with personal conflict because they agree to timelines that are unrealistic. You can manage this by changing roles. Play the role of the manager and gather the information, and then play the role of the consultant who is to deliver the work. What other commitments and obligations will you have to be unreliable for if you provide an aggressive timeline?

Remember, to be reliable you need to use honest and accurate information before you commit.

Dealing with Test-Retest Reliability (Over Time)

This type of reliability is when testing the same person results in the same outcome over time. As a consultant, when our client is asking us a question, it is important to fully understand the context of that question. Early in my career I had a client that asked me a question, and I was nodding my head as I listened. At the end of the question, they left thinking that I was in agreement and giving them a positive or yes answer. I was actually nodding my head to indicate that I understood what they were saying. When my response to the question was no, the client was furious, and I needed to do some patch up work as I lost a little bit of trust.

This can often happen when our clients give a slightly different variation of the same question. It's okay to ask questions back to confirm what they are asking. If you have answered a similar question before, state that. You can say something like, "Last Thursday, Jim asked me a similar question." Then repeat the question as you remember it so they get a context for what you had discussed. Then, provide your answer. Make sure there is some dialogue between you and the client.

There are consultants who feel that some clients are trying to trip them up and cause conflict. I have been on engagements where it is clear that there is internal fighting between departments as well as contempt for the consulting firm and the consultants working for the client. However, this is clearly the exception and not the rule. In almost all cases, any conflict between consultants and their clients is due to fear and worry about the unknown. Our clients want us to help them solve their problems, so having dialogue and building rapport with our clients is the best way to do this.

When we ask the client the same question but receive different answers, this is often a sign that the client may not fully understand the process. Or perhaps, we've asked the question a slightly different way, and maybe the client has gathered more information from the previous question. One other reason could be that there may be some contradictions in the business process.

Previously I mentioned that as a consultant, our job is to try to dig up as many contradictions as we can with our clients. This allows us to fully serve them and deliver the best product and service that we can. Explore the contradictions by asking lots of questions. Let them walk you through the steps of the process, and better yet, if you can watch the live process in progress, you will get a better idea of what is occurring.

Dealing with Internal-Consistency Reliability (Across Items)

Internal-consistency reliability is based on testing different items, possibly by asking similar but different questions, which should result in a similar answer. One way that consultants can use this is often reframing the question or the response back to the client. This can be done in the form of either a question or a statement to make sure that the response is accurate based on the intent of the question or test. Using double negatives or varying the words used will confirm the reliability of the information that we are receiving.

This is a natural way to ask questions if one is skeptical. We don't need to have animosity and skepticism with our clients; however, we must not just shrug our shoulders and take all answers at face value.

The reason we use these forms of reliability testing is that we must deliver the best product for our clients. There is no excuse to say that one of their employees told us something incorrect or we assumed something based on some information. We must do our due diligence and get the correct information.

Dealing with Uncertainty, Risk and Reliability

In the previous chapter we discussed uncertainty related to risk and how it affects reliability. Sometimes when an event occurs that we are unprepared for, individuals may just say, "how was I supposed to know." You can build reliability and trust with your client by being aware of the types of risk uncertainty which will allow you to plan, avoid or mitigate the impact of uncertainty. This also differentiates you from other consultants who don't use this approach of managing risk and uncertainty.

Our personal lives and professional lives tend to blend into each other. I recommend distinguishing between each form of uncertainty into two subcategories which are Professional and Personal. The Professional subcategory is our obligations and expectations with our client. This may be identifying uncertainty while in our role as a consultant. The Personal subcategory is used to manage uncertainty as a consultant with how it affects our personal lives.

The most effective tool that a person can use when evaluating uncertainty is being curious and asking questions. This will help unpack any potential uncertainties and provide information that others may have. It also prompts our creativity to develop better solutions. The better the question the better the answer. My recommendation for all consultants regardless of your age and experience is to continue developing your ability to ask great questions.

Dealing with Known-Knowns

Since we are fully aware of events that are in this category and by definition these events have no uncertainty this is the most straightforward item to deal with. However, this is also the easiest area to lose reliability. To properly manage this form of uncertainty consultants need to properly set expectations with their clients.

In the Professional category of known-knowns, I recommend not assuming your client has the same level of knowledge that you do. As a consultant a large part of your role is to help your client navigate unfamiliar situations and be able to predict where problem areas may lie. Look for signs of missing information with your client's plan. Listen to what your client says and what resources they use during your project. Watch for signs that show your client has missed something or has put too much or too little importance in a particular area of their business.

Having known-knowns is more than just communicating the week that you'll take vacation. Your job is to transfer knowledge to your client so they can be successful.

In regard to the Personal category of known-knowns I've found the best time to put the information into action is as soon as you are aware of the event. This reduces personal stress and allows you to free up mental space by developing and communicating a plan.

In the 2006 movie *RV*, the main character played by Robin Williams and his family are taking a vacation in the country in a recreational vehicle. Williams' character is a consultant who does not tell his boss that he is on vacation nor does he tell his family that he still needs to work. The comedy has many situations where Williams is trying to manage family time while also doing work and meeting deadlines. Of course, the character is not able to do anything right and loses trust with both his family, employer and the client.

This situation has been played out too many times to count. Don't lose trust in yourself by overbooking your time and thinking you can juggle lots of competing tasks at the same time. The best way to deal with this is to be honest and plan out what can be achieved. We often have to do a juggling act however losing reliability and trust to known-knowns is foolish because we are aware of the event and can properly plan for it.

Dealing with Known-Unknowns

This type of uncertainty is when we know an event will occur, we just don't know when or where it will occur. For instance, during the course of a project some people will be ill. The project plan should take into account that someone will be ill, you just don't know who and you don't know when or how long they will be sick. But this is predictable and therefore a certain number of days should be built into any plan to account for this predictive event. This is part of contingency planning.

In our Professional category we know that timelines will slip or due dates will be missed. This is not something we put into a project plan however we need to be mentally prepared for these types of events. To be prepared for a flexible timeline, always be organized and ready to move work that is planned in the future to today. This will allow you to keep tasks moving forward and not lose the available time. You will gain trust and reliability by being able to move tasks around as required by various factors.

Our Personal category also requires us to be flexible. However, the best consultants are most often the hardest on themselves. Many will get frustrated if they get ill, or if family requirements interrupt work. Be mentally prepared for events that will ultimately cause distractions. You're a human being and stuff happens. You will actually build confidence knowing you are prepared if something happens because it undoubtedly will.

Dealing with Unknown-Knowns

Unknown-knowns are events where others have information that we do not have. As stated earlier we should assume that we may not be getting the most accurate information. This doesn't mean that people are purposely withholding information, although it could be the case. Most often though people underestimate the importance of the information, it doesn't come to mind or they don't have enough of the information to fully understand and explain it.

Know as a consultant that you will likely have to rework and add newfound information into your solution. There's no need to be frustrated at performing rework. How you handle these situations will separate you from the consultants who get angry because they have some rework to do.

In our Personal category it is not as apparent that you will withhold information from yourself. However, this is where being honest with yourself comes in. I've seen individuals beat themselves up because they knew something but didn't act on it. I've found it's best to operate like two different people. You are the manager of yourself and you're also the consultant. Even if you work for a company if you can view your two roles you may find success in this area. One role being the manager who is obligated to provide support, administer, reward and discipline the consultant. The second role being the consultant who is required to meet the objectives laid out by the manager. We call this parenting ourselves but I find it important to see me playing two different roles.

This approach also helps when you need to have a difficult conversation with your client. Let's say you need to have a week off due to an unforeseen event. When speaking with your client you can play the role as the manager and act the same way that you would deal with this issue for another consultant. When you get really good at this then you can almost negotiate anything because you have your best interest in mind.

Dealing with Unknown-Unknowns
This form of uncertainty is based on the theory that we lack information that would lead us to believe that a risk or event could occur. These are the situations that seem to come out of the blue without warning.

However, business continuity plans should take into account events that are unforeseeable. For instance, the emergence of COVID-19 would fall into this category. It could be argued that no one could have predicted this virus or planned for the impact of such an event. However, we have had major viruses that have impacted us before, albeit not to this extent.

Unless you're a consultant that is specifically working on a business continuity type of project you may not be faced with this issue. However, I do recommend spending time thinking about ways that your client can continue working if an unforeseen event occurs. I have been pulled into meetings where a fire impacted a client's location. The plan was to determine how to keep some of the operations running and support the families affected by the fire. Being creative and letting your mind think of ways of dealing with unpredictable issues can help your client and your career.

On the Personal category planning for unknown-unknowns may seem silly which is why most people don't take on this task. However, I strongly recommend that you plan for an unknown event. You can use current situations to help you plan. When COVID-19 struck I used some of the planning that people use for earthquakes to better prepare my family. As a consultant ask yourself, if you aren't able to get into the office for months could you continue to work? If not, what would you need to do to continue to work?

In 2013 a flood hit the city of Calgary. I was working for a client in Calgary days before the water breached the riverbanks. When the consultants left, we did not return for weeks due to the devastation and damage. But some people did not think through their departure prior to leaving office as the flood waters rose. Some people had chosen to leave their laptops in the office, assuming they would return the following week, rather than taking their laptops home with them. Remote access to systems was very restrictive at this time so those individuals that left their computers were required to find other ways to execute their work.

I worked with another consultant who practiced an exercise of planning for how she would deal with a catastrophic event. She lived in Arizona but had family in Iowa. She planned how many days it would take her to travel using various modes of transportation from Phoenix to the town her sister lived in Iowa.

I found this entire exercise fascinating however there was something even more interesting that came out of this exercise. She was very prepared for when the COVID-19 lockdown occurred. To put context around this, she was not a doomsday follower, rather she just knew there was a chance of a major event occurring and she wanted to be prepared.

For all four (4) types of uncertainty being flexible and fluid is required. You need to draw on your experience, resourcefulness and be aware of what is occurring around you.

In the words of our dear friend Bruce Lee, "Be like water my friend."

3 Ways to Become More Reliable

1. Set expectations

Often reliability is affected because expectations are not properly set. Make sure as a consultant that you are explicit with what is expected between you and the client. This goes both ways, as they are relying on us and we are relying on them. If there is any ambiguity, then confirm. Take the time to understand exactly what needs to be done, when it needs to be done, and the quality of the final product the client is expecting. Ask questions like, "What will that look like", "How will we know that the goal has been met", or "What does success look like?"

These questions will help set the expectations for you and others.

One of the biggest culprits of this is impatience. Often people will give unclear instructions, and as consultants, we may not question or even explain things properly when we're giving instructions. This is frequently due to time constraints, distractions, and even not wanting to hurt someone's feelings.

Be explicit in what needs to be done and document the expectations. It's important that people be treated like adults and be given the proper amount of responsibility. However, we should not assume that everyone understands what needs to be done or the quality of the work expected.

I once worked for a client where one of their managers was always very unclear on his expectations. I thought the manager was just in a rush or didn't know what he wanted. But as I began to do some work for this manager, I began to see that his vague instructions were purposeful. The reason being that if something was missed, he would have someone to blame or point to as the reason it happened.

What I began to do was ask more questions of him and be more explicit in what was required. My goal was to validate his thoughts and requirements; however, he became very annoyed when I would ask questions. I would also follow up with an email explaining what we had discussed. Documenting and emailing the notes from the meeting came in handy many times, as the expectations were documented and he had an opportunity to respond to the email.

Of course, this strained our relationship, as it became apparent to me that he felt that it was inappropriate that I would clarify what he was requiring. My approach was not to cause conflict or attack his leadership; however, running off on a fool's errand is not an approach I recommend to any consultant.

My recommendation when things become unclear is to be explicit and document what is discussed.

2. Learn to say no

Most consultants fall into one of two camps. The first is the group that constantly says, "This is out of scope, and we will not do it." They constantly try to squeeze the scope and work that the client asks so that the consultants or consulting firm deliver less throughout the engagement. The second group is one that always says, "Yes, I can do that." I naturally fall into the latter group and do everything I can to make the client happy. Now it's important to deliver all that you can for your client, but it's critical to know when you just cannot deliver what they are asking for. The cause of not being able to say "No" is often due to our personalities. This stems from not wanting to let people down. Learning to say "No" in a professional manner or to reset expectations is important.

If a client asks for you to turn something around in the next two days and you had committed to some vacation time with your family, then you need to either renegotiate the vacation time or the work with a client. Find out how critical the client's work is.

I had a client once that would always have priority-one or critical issues and tasks. When you completed one, they would just bump up the severity-two issues to become severity one. The problem with this approach is that, over time, nothing was critical because everything was critical. All tasks would end up being worked in a methodical approach regardless of if it was time sensitive or not. What the client needed to learn was to say no within their own process.

We must all remember that when we say yes to something, we in turn are saying no to something else. We only have so much time in the day, so if we are agreeing to perform functions or agreeing to timelines that are unmanageable, we in turn are agreeing to not do something else.

Do what you can to open your schedule up so that you are available for your clients. That means staying on top of administrative, training, and other activities that may be sacrificed in order to achieve your client objectives.

Lombardi Time
Coach Vince Lombardi of the Green Bay Packers had a rule for his players. They had to be at their meetings and practices 15 minutes early. That's because 15 minutes

early was his definition of being on time. Arriving later than 15 minutes prior to the meeting meant his players were late.

It can be tough as consultants to run from meeting to meeting and be on time. It can also be difficult to juggle all the requirements and demands during an engagement with a client. Adding to it, we have personal lives that we are trying to live. Let's face it: We are just human beings, and we can only do so much.

But we need to complete the things we say we will, when we promised. This means having control over our time and what we are committing to. Be reasonable with the deliverables that you promise to complete for your client. Also, make sure you are booking time for yourself and your personal commitments.

I recommend learning time management skills and continually working on developing these skills. There are great courses available and some information is included in the appendix of this book.

Overall, the client is expecting you to deliver what you promised and at the time you promised it. Do your best to meet these commitments. This is a continual effort to keep all of our conflicting objectives in line but it can be accomplished.

3. Provide options and recommendations

This is part of Consulting 101; however, many consultants will not provide options and recommendations to their clients. To be reliable and generate competence, always provide options and recommendations to your clients. Status quo is always an option, however, you should use common sense when providing this type of recommendation. Clients are not paying you to tell them to stay where they are. Not making a major change may be the correct recommendation; however, you must provide some guidance and suggestions to deal with the pain of the problem they are trying to correct.

I once was with a client when their support team could not fix a problem. The solution they provided their client was that they just had to live with the errors as the support team was unable to determine the cause or fix the issue. This type of recommendation is not acceptable. Even if they could not fix the problem, they were obligated to find someone to help resolve the issue.

It can be very difficult to go on the record and provide a recommendation, especially when there can be political fallout from recommending one option over another. These are situations where you may upset a decision maker if you recommend a solution. You can also set off a firestorm by presenting what you believe is right.

To deal with this, I recommend having some conversations off the record and in private. A consultant can be as much a lobbyist and politician as they can be a technical problem solver. The best consultants are able to determine when to put the politician hat on and maneuver some choppy waters.

This is where the relationships that you built will serve you. Also, your competence, authenticity, and empathy, which is discussed in this book, will help you through some turbulent times.

The reason this lesson is in reliability and not any of the other sections is that the clients are looking to you for a consistent, reliable, and often stoic approach to guiding them through their challenges. Clients aren't paying you to read a map; they are paying you to guide them through the journey from where they are to where they want to be. When you can reliably perform this kind of guidance, you will be a highly sought-after resource.

Reliability and Three-Way Trust

Practicing the steps to continually demonstrate reliability will reinforce the three directions of trust; how the client trusts you, how you trust the client and how you trust yourself. Reliability is the third component of trust and developing trusted advisor status with your client.

Trust Exercise – Reliability

Use the information in this section to analyze where you and others develop trust through reliability. Also, you'll be able to review relationships where trust is lacking due to ineffective reliablity.

By developing the skills to review relationships in this way you will be able to identify missing elements which add conflict and pressure to interactions. It will also allow you the ability to better recognize others that have skills that align with your goals and objectives which enable meaningful and rewarding relationships.

Reliablity is one skill that all consultants should aspire to develop and demonstrate. It is a virtue that all relationships require and is skill that is sought out by all clients.

Taking the Next Step: Giving Back

In this chapter, you've learned methods of developing reliability. I request that you share what you've learned with others. Please pass along any new methodologies or approaches you've learned or write articles on the information. There are three main results that occur from giving back to others in this way:

1. You become the example

When you give back to others by sharing information, you become the example. In regard to reliability, you will be *the* example of dependability. Your name and image will be synonymous with this resulting in better client engagements.

2. You get grace

When you teach others and act as an example of reliability in a compassionate manner then you are provided grace when external factors impact your reliability on occasion. Be caring toward others when their reliability waivers but provide guidance so that others can improve.

3. You teach yourself

When you give back to others, you reinforce the skills of reliability. You also imbed those skills as part of yourself. You become more reliable because you are reliable, and since you are teaching others and giving back, you become even more so.

Section 4: Empathy

Chapter 10: Empathy and Trust

"When you show deep empathy toward others, their defensive energy goes down, and positive energy replaces it. That's when you can get more creative in solving problems." -Stephen Covey

During the spring of 1997, Manitoba, Canada experienced one of the worst floods in its history. As the flood was just beginning, a small trucking company that hauled livestock stepped up their game and started hauling livestock that was at risk in the flood area. The trucking operation worked as much as they could, moving cattle, hogs, horses, and other animals to higher and safer areas. Much of this they did without charging many of the farmers. Why would this small trucking operation do this? Because they felt empathy for the fear, worry, and anxiety that their neighbors (who happened to be farmers) were going through. They contributed what they could to help those in need.

After the flood resided and things got back to normal, the farmers in the area chose one trucking company to haul their livestock: the one that helped them through the flood. Even farmers who used to haul their own animals chose to hire them. This trucking company is now very large and seemed to expand exponentially almost overnight.

The owner didn't choose to overcharge for a service and take advantage of a situation to make money. In fact, he did the opposite. He elected not to charge many farmers who could not afford to hire him to save their animals.

There was no guarantee that his company would reap the reward of this empathy. But I am sure that the owner of the trucking company would have done it regardless, as I am sure he felt it was the right thing to do because of his empathy.

What We Think Empathy Is

Empathy differs from sympathy. Often when someone thinks they have empathy, they are really showing sympathy. Sympathy is sorrow or pity for someone else's hardships. Feeling sorry for someone can create feelings of pity. Feelings of pity can be produced when we recognize someone is in a difficult or unfortunate position which is worse than ours.

Before I had children I thought I was empathizing with parents when they experienced hardship with their children. It wasn't until I had my own children that I realized I was just expressing sympathy. There was no doubt that my feelings for the hardships that parents were experiencing changed to empathy when I became a parent, as I could feel the pain they felt when something unfavorable happened to their children. Similarly, many consultants express sympathy for their clients when they are experiencing hardships. It's another form of feeling sorry for your client. However, the greatest consultants experience empathy. They feel what their client is feeling. They use words like "we" and "us" when speaking with the client, just as if they are part of their company. They also can see out in the future, long past the end of the contract. They imagine the positive impact that their efforts are making on the client and the benefits the client receives in the future.

If you don't believe this is possible, think of a teacher you had in your past that really believed in you. They saw what you could be. They weren't just teaching the curriculum and getting the school year in. They saw you as what you could be: a successful, productive, contributing adult.
Great consultants do this same thing for their clients. They see what they can be and help them get there. The consultant is part of the team.

What Empathy Actually Is

Empathy is the ability to understand and share the feelings of another person. It's the ability to put yourself in someone else's shoes. This is the beginning of being able to care for another human being. As consultants a big responsibility we have is to have empathy for our clients and their businesses.

One thing I try to do is to ask myself, "If this was my company, what would I do?" This allows me to put myself in the position of my client and think about the challenges, stress, and pain they may be going through. This frame of mind puts me in a state to better empathize with my client, so that I can start to feel what they feel.

Empathy is also the first step to being part of the team. We can't fake this level of feeling; however, certain words are indicators to how someone may feel about their client. This is not a scientific approach, but I have found the words people use indicate what they are thinking. When a consultant uses the word "we" when referring to the client, as in, "We need to resolve this issue," the consultant is indicating that they are part of the team. If another consultant uses the word "you," as in, "You need to resolve this issue," they may not see themselves as part of the team.

Someone may ask, why doesn't pity create empathy? I'll answer that with a question, have you ever been in an unfortunate situation with another person? Did you feel sympathy or pity for the other person? I am almost certain the answer is no. That is because you are also experiencing the same unfortunate situation.

To have empathy you must understand and feel what the other person or people are feeling.

Why Empathy Is Important for Consultants

Quite often, empathy is one of the skills that many consultants put on the back burner. This is due to focusing on technical skills and also being emotionally, mentally, and physically exhausted from the nature of consulting.

As consultants, it's our job to hold a standard of empathy. This is what makes us human and not just a brain on a stick for our clients. It also builds deep rapport, which creates a strong bond. My most memorable projects are ones where the empathy was deep between me and my client.

To make an impact in your career and in this world, you require empathy.

Empathy Can Soften the Hardest Stone
Empathy can be the driver of all the other categories of trust. When asking a child why they don't trust someone else, they often will say the person just doesn't care. What they're really referring to is the fact that the person shows little to no empathy toward them.

If you hear your client state that someone doesn't care, this is what they're referring to. I've said this multiple times before: Clients are not just hiring us for a technical solution. In fact, most consultants don't want to be playing in the technical solution pond as technical solutions are easy to develop. As a consultant you want to be functioning with empathy toward your client.

Although this is the fourth category of trust, this is the ultimate driver of becoming a trusted advisor for your client. I've been doing work for one client since 2003. I've always had in my mind that I could sit in front of the CEO and tell her that every decision or recommendation that I've provided was for the best interest of the company and not for the best interest of me or my company. That doesn't mean that every single recommendation I provided was successful or turned out to be right. But it was the recommendation that I thought was correct at that time with the information that I was provided.

Using this approach allows me to think, *If this was my company, what would I do?* By doing this my actions and recommendations contain care, empathy, and compassion. I begin to feel what the client feels with these decisions. Having said that, it's very important that consultants do not internalize the stresses and anxiety that the client is feeling. What this means is that we must take on their problems and act like they're our own. However, we must remain independent and objective to provide the best decision making, solutions, and recommendations for our clients.

I use the analogy that when a doctor is performing surgery on a patient, the doctor has to take on the patient's problem. The doctor has to care about the procedure as if she was operating on a family member. But the doctor also must not internalize the stress that the patient is under. She remains an objective professional while performing the entire operation. This is a balancing act that all consultants must strive to develop.

Transactional vs. Relational Relationships

Too often consultants rely on transactional relationships with their clients. This means these relationships are referred to as "quid pro quo," which translated means, "this for that." These types of relationships have very little empathy as both parties or one of the parties feels that the relationship is based on the transaction and not on the relationship.

Relational relationships are based on empathy and mutual respect. These types of relationships provide the ability to make mistakes, work through problems together, and build camaraderie that is almost not existent in a transactional relationship. Empathy lives in the relational relationships where we see each other as human beings, and we support each other. This is where trusted advisors function.

Relational relationships provide a meaningful, fulfilling, and rewarding career. These relationships are more profitable, take less time to manage, and administer and provide opportunities for both the client and the consultants.

We Recognize Empathy in Others

My wife's pregnancy with my son had many complications. On three occasions I flew into my client site on Monday morning only to have to fly home Monday night because of a health concern with my wife. I had just started this project with this client and had very little history with them. The project manager at the time whose name was Shirley always supported me when I needed to return home. In fact, the three main people I worked with on this project supported me when I needed to return home. Shirley, Terry, and Scott never questioned why I was leaving and always encouraged me to return home to provide support for my wife. They never made me feel guilty for leaving or acted like they would be put out.

The empathy they showed me during that time generated years of goodwill. I would often take phone calls at inconvenient times to provide guidance and advice when they required it. I know I could call any three of them today, and they would help me, the same as I would help them whenever they needed it.

Others Recognize Empathy in Us

During one of the complications of the pregnancy, my wife and I went to one of the local hospitals in the city we lived in. As with many hospital emergency rooms, it can look at times like a civil war hospital. The emergency room was packed, and there were people sleeping on gurneys in the hallways because the hospital was overcrowded.

As I sat in the hallway with my wife (who was one of the ones sitting and sleeping in the hallway), the doors opened from the emergency waiting room back to the hospital. On the gurney was a little boy, possibly a year-and-a-half old. He had tubes coming out of his mouth and nose and tubes going into his arms and his chest. The site was something that hit you, as the boy was tiny and barely noticeable on this big, long stretcher. As in most waiting rooms, the great majority of people were in pain or they're 100% focused on supporting the loved one that they were with. As this little boy was rolled in on a stretcher through the emergency room, every person in the waiting room looked at the boy with a level of empathy that has stuck with me to this day. One older gentleman who seemed to be in his eighties was walking by in obvious pain from his own ailments. This was a grizzled, weathered, and obviously sick man. But when he saw the boy, his own pain seemed to leave him as he focused on the young boy. The look on the elderly man's face showed nothing but compassion and empathy for the situation the young child was in.

What hit me was the change of energy that occurred in that area. What had previously felt like pain and misery increased to a level of empathy and compassion. When we are the providers of empathy toward others, we can change a situation of pain into one of recovery.

We Recognize Empathy in Ourselves

If you've gotten this far in the book, you're already considered a high achiever. A 2019 survey showed that 27% of Americans did not read a book in the previous year. Of those that earn $75,000 or more, 86% have read at least one book compared to only 67% of those that earned less than $50,000. It is also estimated that 57% of books that a reader starts are never completed.

Total percentage of Americans that did not read a book the past year	27%
Total percentage of American that read at least one book with income over $75,000	86%
Total percentage of American that read at least one book with income under $50,000	67%
Total percentage of books started that aren't read to completion	57%

If we continue on the premise that you are a high achiever, you potentially have high expectations for yourself. High expectations also bring on the potential to push ourselves. When we push ourselves we tend to show less self-empathy.

We're all raised differently by different parents and in different environments. Some people use the same techniques to parent themselves as their parents demonstrated for them. Others choose the opposite approach. Others go through a lifetime of self-improvement to try to change the way they manage themselves.

Just like authenticity is a lifetime journey of finding ourselves, participating in new experiences, and questioning our beliefs, empathy is also a lifelong journey. There are times where we need to kick ourselves in the pants to get going and other times we need to show compassion towards ourselves.

This may be the most challenging balancing act of empathy you will experience in your life. We witness those who give themselves permission to have low expectations and miss every goal they want to achieve. We also are surrounded by high achievers who seem to have endless energy and more time in the day to achieve more than us.

As consultants, our demands on ourselves can be the biggest challenge. To properly be able to build competence, be authentic to ourselves and others, and be reliable, we must practice self-empathy.

Often, I've noticed the lack of empathy we have toward others is driven from the lack of empathy we have towards ourselves. Routinely I will see parents put demands on their children due to a lack of empathy the parents show themselves. Often this comes from a feeling of inadequacy, missed opportunities, and wanting to punish ourselves due to guilt and remorse. This is one of the hardest lessons I've had to learn, and I am challenged by it every day. My children are not me. The remorse and guilt that we feel from our past should not be used as a tool to motivate others. We need to be a coach to those closest to us.

Show yourself some compassion. You're over 75% done with this book, and that is better than most people. Make sure you complete the book and put into practice what you've learned about yourself. You can be your best coach and teacher.

Chapter 11: What the Experts Say About Empathy

"I think we all have empathy. We may not have enough courage to display it." -Maya Angelou

Empathy Is Natural to Human Beings

Human beings aren't as self-serving as common belief would lead us to think. Our survival relies on participating in the group. When you hear a baby start crying, you'll notice that other babies around will also start crying. This is a response to the distress they are witnessing from another person. Someone else is upset which makes them upset.

In his book, *Super Cooperators*, Martin A. Nowak states that there are five ways cooperators gain an edge. It is through:

- Direct reciprocity
  - I help someone, and they will help me
- Indirect reciprocity
  - I help someone, and someone else will help me
- Spatial selection
  - clusters of cooperators, gain an advantage
- Group selection
  - group of cooperators, gains an advantage
- Kin selection
  - family of cooperators gain an advantage

Cooperators are not self-serving; however, they are ambitious and are willing to help others out along the way, as well as willing to accept others' help.

To be a true cooperator, we must be empathetic toward others as well as ourselves.

Theory of Mind

Theory of mind is the cognitive ability to attribute mental states to yourself and others. In layman's terms, you are able to define the mental state of another person. Of course, most of us are not psychologists or psychiatrists, so we actually do not have the training to officially define someone's mental state, but socially, we are able to make that definition.

Most of us use the simulation theory, sometimes called the "empathy theory." Robert Gordon suggested that we can predict others' behavior by answering the question, "What would I do in that person's situation?"

In his article, "Theory of Mind," Alvin I. Goldman identifies that Wilhelm Dilthey wrote of understanding others through a process of feeling with others, re-experiencing their mental states, or putting oneself into their shoes. This is what most of us do when empathizing with others.

One obstacle that consultants run into when working with their clients is that they have often not experienced some of the stress, changes, and trauma that the individuals and employees at their client sites are going through. We must draw on others experiences to be able to empathize with them.

One example of this is that for years, I believed that employees of companies should just accept that change is inevitable and not fight the change or feel anxiety when it comes. Then, I had to taste my own medicine. What happened to me was a client of mine was changing managers that I was to report to. The new manager's name was Mike, and I was to meet him the following day. I had a hard time sleeping that night and was very nervous and anxious about this change. It was at that moment that I realized the stress that our clients are under when they have to experience change.

From that moment on, I had a different amount of empathy and compassion toward my clients while they were implementing some form of change. Fortunately, in my case, I got along with Mike and actually ended up working with him at a different client as well.

Two Types of Empathy

Cognitive Empathy

Cognitive empathy is the ability to understand how someone else feels. When one imagines how someone else is feeling, this is cognitive empathy. This is more of a mental task, as we attempt to put ourselves in someone else's position. This is an important part of being a human being, as we may not have the personal experience to draw on when someone goes through a difficult time. With cognitive empathy, we are able to generate empathy by imagining how the other person feels.

Our family had experienced a devastating loss when my niece decided to end her own life. As our family was together trying to understand what had happened, a confusing, surreal feeling came over me. Then I remembered one of my best friends named Guy. Guy lost his brother the same way around twenty years earlier. I was very close to his family. I said to myself, "This is what Guy and his family felt." Prior to this realization, I only had cognitive empathy for Guy and his family. But after that moment, I moved from cognitive empathy to emotional empathy.

Emotional Empathy

Emotional empathy is the sharing of an emotional experience. This drives us to want to help another person.

Social psychology researchers Hodges and Davis describe emotional empathy in three parts:

1. Feeling the same emotion as the other person
2. Feeling our own distress in response to their pain
3. Feeling compassion toward the other person

Emotional empathy moves us to do something to help others. Our clients need us to have emotional empathy for their situations. The consultants that have this not only deliver a better product, but they'll also be asked back more frequently by their clients.

Emoto's Water Experiment

Dr. Masaru Emoto conducted a number of experiments to study the effects of prayer, words, and the environment had on the physical structure of water. Emoto hired photographers to take pictures of water as it was being frozen and forming the crystalline structures. A crystalline structure is any structure of ions, molecules, or atoms that are held together in an ordered, three-dimensional arrangement. Emoto wrote positive phrases on one group of containers and negative phrases on another group of containers that stored the crystalline structures.

The results were astounding. The water that had positive messages on it was more symmetrical and aesthetically pleasing than the water that had negative writings on it.

The reason the study is so important is that the thoughts and words we use when thinking of other human beings will impact how they react to us and how they behave. Our bodies are around 60% water. So, if amassing negative thoughts or words will affect water inside containers, imagine the effect it has on human beings?

Fairness and Cooperation

There are various studies that show that fairness motives affect the behavior of many individuals. This is also true of cooperation. However, individuals may behave differently based on different situations. In their article, "A Theory of Fairness, Competition, and Cooperation" Ernst Fehr and Klaus M. Schmidt writes, "There are situations in which the standard self-interest model is unambiguously refuted. However, in other situations the predictions of this model seem to be very accurate."

What this means is that not all individuals are driven by self-interest; however, those same individuals may not always be driven by fairness and cooperation at all times either. This affects empathy as we need to be aware that our clients may behave differently throughout a project and may behave differently based on the impact to themselves and others.

The best consultants are able to see this complicated duplicity in others and provide support and understanding to those around them.

Chapter 12: How to Become More Empathetic

"Empathy begins with understanding life from another person's perspective. Nobody has an objective experience of reality. It's all through our own individual prisms." -Sterling K. Brown

I grew up in a rural part of Manitoba, Canada which was very impoverished. The people who lived in this area had a toughness about them. Not just a physical toughness, but also an emotional toughness. Most were of Ukrainian descent. When one of my best friends passed away at 44 years old, we were told a story by the priest at the funeral. He said that in Ukraine, some churches would bring women to funerals who could cry at will. The purpose of this was, as the women began to weep, everyone else in the church would also start to cry. This would allow those in attendance to release their sorrow and pain.

My son and I experienced something like this at a funeral we attended. A baseball coach of my son's passed away in a car accident at age 41. George had a wife and four young children. After arriving we sat there quietly for about 45 minutes. Most people looked calm and were waiting for the priest to start the service. Then, an elderly gentleman walked in and went to the casket. He started crying and speaking in a foreign language. He was speaking loudly and crying. He hugged and kissed some family members and then sat down. The church was quiet. People were holding back tears, including myself. If one other person began to cry, everyone would be weeping.

I thought about this unique idea and my childhood. I thought about why people become hardened. I grew up in an area with less than a thousand people. There were many accidents. There was a girl in my sister's class who had an accident with a tractor that resulted in breaking many of her bones. The father of two boys at my school was pulled into a grain auger and needed to be cut out with a torch. Another man down the road from us lost his arm in a baler. The man who lived across the road from us lost many fingers as a child cutting wood. There were too many accidents to count.

Anyone who had their childhood prior to the late 1980's had never heard the term "tough love" as a child. Everyone I knew experienced difficult situations throughout their childhood so there was no need to artificially create scenarios where tough love needed to be taught. Having said that, I know every person reading this book has faced difficulties and challenges. If you also grew up in the country or a rural area, you probably also have stories like mine where people were hurt or tragically killed. Urban centers have other hazards that may have caused a breakdown in compassion such as car accidents, crimes, and other events. For others, times may have been financially difficult or there may have been untold challenges occurring in the home. And there may have felt like there was little opportunity available to you or others around you.

The reason I included this in this section is that often, high achievers have a very difficult time with empathy. They struggle with the concept of empathy and compassion because they often feel that people should just get to it and put emotions behind them. High achievers often operate with a tough love mindset knowing the world will hand out enough punishment to being an average person to their knees. They've adopted the mindset of being able to take punishment to achieve their goals and they feel everyone around them should be do the same. This approach desensitizes the high achiever from those around them resulting in conflict and strained relationships. Not all high achievers operate this way however it is not uncommon to find high achievers acting unempathetically.

I would love to tell you that if you act this way or that way, you'll be empathetic. However, I often feel like telling those who have challenges around me to shake it off or toughen up. To just wrap that injured limb up and get back up. But I know deep down, that is not the answer. It's not the answer that our paying clients are looking for, and it's not the answer that another human being needs to hear in a time when they are in pain.

The answer is to be empathetic, sincere and compassionate. But I would be lying if I was to imply that I always show compassion and empathy. After realizing this about myself, I try and work on methods to "wear off" the calluses that have built up. We've all seen and experienced hardships. Some people have experienced catastrophic hardships, and so have our clients. I suggest we all try and work on the positive side and function with compassion and empathy.

12 Ways to Become More Empathetic

1. See them as a child
In my book, *The Consultant's Code,* I wrote a section called "The Baby Needs to be Fed." This was in regard to how sometimes, other people can start acting aggressively, but if you picture them as a baby that needs to be fed, you can start to look at them differently.

With empathy, it's the same way. We often look at people as a group rather than as individuals. Next time you're out in public, look at each person as an individual. Without being creepy, look at a person long enough to see and try to feel what they're about. Often you can see the turmoil and pain that another human being is covering up. Other times you can see the humor or silliness of a person just by watching them.

This creates empathy toward the human being and builds a connection to each other. If you're able to do this consistently or frequently, others will know that you are an empathetic person. It will come out naturally.

2. Allow others to learn on their own

Consultants routinely get into situations where they feel that they must be the savior and save people from themselves. There are times when we must allow our clients a chance at learning a lesson and experiencing a consequence on their own. We should never set them up to fail; however, sometimes we all need to learn through consequences. Perhaps the client needed to learn a lesson or learn new skills and the route they took, albeit not something that we would have suggested, was the route they had to take. And who knows? Maybe they teach us a new path.

We've all had times in our lives when someone else was meddling in something we wanted to do. Perhaps the other person knew better than we did, but we still wanted to do it our way. If you're a parent, you likely do this with your own children. I know I do!

I was advising a client that was to take on a very large project. Even though most of their internal resources had never worked on a project of that size, they chose to do the project alone without external consultant help. The end client was a government department. I have had the opportunity to work on a number of government projects, and I know at times they can be very challenging. My recommendation to the client was to have some sort of external consultants involved that have this type of experience. The client still chose to do it on their own.

This was difficult for me to watch, as I could predict many of the pitfalls that the team was going to run into. However, I also knew the client was going to do whatever they wanted to. In fact, the more I advised, the more they would likely resist. I needed to let them do it on their own if they chose to and be ready if they called for my help.

3. I told you so

"I told you so" can come in many forms. It can come in the form of a blatant statement, questioning who agreed to this, shaking your head with eye rolling. The very best consultants are able to avoid, "I told you so." This is difficult because often, consultants bring in a lot of emotions when it comes to their recommendations. Eliminate your emotional connection to your thoughts, decisions, and recommendations. Also disconnect your emotional connection to decisions and recommendations you have not been involved with. Punishing our clients and other people's poor decisions is an easy way to lose trust. We should always assume that decisions were made with the best intentions and information that was available at that time.

4. Empathy is not manipulation

Most adults have had situations in their lives where they have had a relationship with someone that seemed to be caring to only end up finding out they're manipulative. It might be a boss that seemed to be concerned about your career but then punished you and gave you the cold shoulder when you changed jobs or left the company.

I once worked with a consultant who was like Jekyll and Hyde. He was very caring and engaged during workshops, meetings, and in front of the client. But I saw moments behind the scenes where the behavior was 180 degrees different.

We were struggling with getting all of the information that we needed to gather for the requirements for a very large utility company. He and I sat down and started to discuss how we would get it back on track. I gave a few ideas before he interrupted me and said, "I don't give a F*#* if we have to stay till 3 in the morning to get this information. But the clients are going to stay until we get all of it." I saw the bully behavior come out from him.

I found this very interesting because there were a few people on the project that shared with me later that they had a feeling they could not trust him as soon as they met him. I never did share with them that story, however, I found it funny that they were able to notice that they were unable to trust him right away.

5. Let others feel what they feel
Too often we judge whether others' emotional responses are valid or justified for the situation. If we feel the responses are not justified we give indications or react in a way to communicate that the emotions are not wanted. However, one approach is to allow others to feel what they feel. Give them some time to feel it and then coach them to move on. We coach them to move on by doing just that, moving on. We focus back on the situation at hand, the challenge or issue and start planning a

solution. Do this for yourself and give yourself permission to feel the emotion and then move on and get back to work.

6. Disagree without being disagreeable

This came from one of the greatest consultants in history. Coach John Wooden used basketball as his business, but had he selected any other line of work, he would have been a phenomenal success. This is because he was quite possibly, in my opinion, one of the best consultants ever.

One of his major thoughts was that people can disagree without being disagreeable. He never had an issue with someone disagreeing with his point of view or challenging his thoughts, however, he did not like it when people took a personal attack at others.

In consulting, this can happen often. I know I have had my share of conflict where the situation became very personal. Looking back, I'm embarrassed and ashamed of how some of those relationships ended up, as well as my behavior in those situations. I still see situations where consultants yell at clients, roll their eyes, interrupt, and show other forms of contempt.

When we disagree with our clients, it's important to attack the problem and the subject matter, not the person. In the end we all want a working solution for the problems. But there is no need to personally attack another person for their thoughts or ideas.

7. Learn to apologize. If you broke it, you bought it

In the, *The Consultant's Code,* I use the phrase, "if you broke it, you bought it." This concept refers to the fact that if you make a mistake, you need to own up to it as soon as you realize you made it. This means apologizing and trying to do what's right to fix the situation.

When you do this, you show the client that you care and that you are empathetic towards them.

8. Accept yourself

When we have difficulty accepting ourselves, we will likely have difficulty accepting others. It is very difficult to have empathy toward another person when you're struggling to show empathy toward yourself.

Margarita Tartakovsky writes an article in *PsychCentral*, called "Therapists Spill: 12 Ways to Accept Yourself." The twelve ways are:
1. Set an intention
2. Celebrate your strengths
3. Consider the people around you
4. Create a support system
5. Forgive yourself
6. Shush your inner critic
7. Grieve the loss of unrealized dreams
8. Perform charitable acts
9. Realize that acceptance is not resignation
10. Speak to your highest self
11. Be kind to yourself
12. Fake it 'til you make it

These steps are not just important for being a consultant but also in your personal life. Work on developing a nature of self-acceptance.

9. Cultivate open mindedness

In Danielle DiPirro's book, *Stay Positive: Daily Reminders from Positively Present*, she identifies seven (7) ways of developing open mindedness. Those methods are:

1. Let go of control
   - Allows you to develop new ideas
2. Experience changes
   - Allows you to develop new beliefs
3. Make yourself vulnerable
   - Puts you at risk and triggers an awakening through fear and exhilaration
4. Make mistakes
   - Failing can help you develop new skills
5. Strengthen yourself
   - Develops new skills from skills you've previously developed
6. Gain confidence
   - Develops a strong sense of self
7. Be honest
   - Develops authenticity

10.   Be sensitive

Being sensitive actually generates credibility because other people realize that you have someone else's interest in mind. Often as consultants we can be so focused on the end result that we may shelf our sensitivity. Remember that our clients and their employees are people. They have feelings, and they're dealing with their own issues and challenges. If you can be the bigger person and leader, you'll have much more rewarding relationships with your clients.

11. Meditate

There are many great books and programs on meditation. I won't go into depth on meditation here, however, meditation will help you become clearer and more focused. Meditation should be done daily, and you will recognize many benefits, including:

1. Reduced stress
2. Increased concentration
3. Increased self-awareness
4. Increased acceptance

The highest performers in business, sports, and media all use meditation. Find a time daily to meditate, and this will help you develop strong habits and empathy toward yourself and your clients.

12. Validate fear, but don't internalize it

Clients will feel better when you listen and show empathy toward them, however, for your own health and theirs, do not internalize their fears.

I think one of the best skills I have as a consultant served me well during the early part of my career. I was able to feel what the client felt. Unfortunately, my inexperience caused me to internalize the feelings of my clients. I often took their stress and made it mine. Very often I would get worked up and show anxiety over the changes, timelines, and resourcing issues the client was facing. As the years went on, I was able to learn to empathize and take on their issues as my own without internalizing the issues.

Do this by defining your roles in different terms. You can call yourself a guide, coach, teacher, an implementer, or facilitator.

Compassion Fatigue: Can You Be *too* Empathetic?

Compassion fatigue is when you become indifferent to those requesting your help due to the frequency of the requests. Compassion fatigue is common in the medical industry, but it also definitely affects many consultants, although it is seldom discussed.

Consultants get tired of helping their clients with what seems to be the same, never-ending tasks. Often consultants have fixed the same problems or explained the same solutions a multitude of times across various clients.

Compassion fatigue will affect our ability to empathize with others.

Susan Fletcher, a psychologist who focuses on helping professionals apply strategies to be successful in their careers, identifies the following five actions as helpful in coping with compassion fatigue:

1. Exercising
2. Maintaining a personal life
3. Having a sense of humor
4. Setting limits between work and home activities
5. Broadening your network

It is important to remember that compassion fatigue exists, and it will affect those of us in consulting as we are helping others throughout our career. Practicing healthy habits is paramount to the success of a consultant as we are often required to shoulder much of the stress and burden for our clients.

Empathy and Three-Way Trust

Demonstrating empathy for yourself and your clients is the fourth component of developing your trusted advisor status. Exercise empathy to strengthen the three directions of trust; how the client trusts you, how you trust the client and how you trust yourself. This will provide a strong solid foundation to support the stress and pressure that we all experience with consulting. This will make you stand out from all other consultants.

Trust Exercise - Empathy

Develop the ability to analyze where you and others nurture trust through empathy. Also, you'll be able to review relationships that are strained due to a lack of empathy.

Having the ability to review relationships in this way will allow you to determine unempathetic behavior that is causing conflict and stress. It will also provide you the ability to better recognize others that have skills that align with your goals and objectives which enable meaningful and rewarding relationships. Take personal responsibility for nurturing empathy in your relationships.

Taking the Next Step: Giving Back

In this chapter, you've learned methods of developing empathy. I request that you share what you've learned with others. Please pass along any new methodologies or approaches you've learned or write articles on the information. There are three main results that occur from giving back to others in this way:

1. You become the example

In a time when people seem to be becoming more disconnected, we need those that demonstrate connectedness such as empathy. Others will notice this and use what you teach them. Being an example of an empathetic human being is something that must be held in high regard.

2. The group evolves

You will be the one that shows that empathy is good, and you will have a more in-touch group. You will find that things around you flow and that the group takes care of each other. This makes our jobs as human beings easier, as we are more in tune with what is occurring around us.

3. The higher power smiles on you

When you are teaching and demonstrating empathy, God (the Universe) smiles and provides more opportunities for you. The higher power wants to see empathy between human beings, and those that are exercising this and teaching others receive more in regard to abundance.

Conclusion

"Never believe that a few caring people can't change the world. For, indeed, that's all who ever have."
-Margaret Mead

Trust Exercise

At the end of each section I explained the trust exercise for each component of trust. I cannot stress enough that the purpose of developing skills related the trust is to improve relationships. Too often tension in relationships cause stress, resulting in lack of trust and ultimately the relationship being discarded. Many of these can be avoided by better aligning our goals and values as we enter relationships. Also, as relationships are strained, having the skills to identify what trust component may be weak allows us to invest in improving, supporting or mitigating the deficiency.

Using the skills taught in *The Trust Paradigm* will not only help you be an even better consultant but it will also improve the relationships that you have in your personal and professional life.

Personal Responsibility

Earlier in the book I discussed how personal responsibility is a foundational value that is linked to each skill related to trust. I encourage you to wake up everyday and tell yourself *"Today, I am taking responsibility for my thoughts, actions and behavior."* Remind yourself throughout the day of your personal responsibility to yourself. Personal responsibility is a foundation of success and those that are successful exercise this daily.

C.A.R.E.

Throughout the book I used the word "care" a number of times to describe aspects of trust. Care spells out the four elements of trust:

C - Credibility
A - Authenticity
R - Reliability
E - Empathy

This not only helps you remember the components of trust but also sums up trust in a single word.

Trust is something that is earned but never owned. We must constantly work on developing trust by caring. Do you care enough to consistently develop credibility? Are you persistent enough to do the hard work and search inside of yourself to determine your authentic self? Are you prepared to live up to your commitments, no matter how difficult, to demonstrate reliability? Do you care enough about others and yourself to nurture empathy even in challenging times?

This is a tall order and the reason why trust can wane so easily. But it is possible to accomplish. In the years to come we need more men, women and children focusing on building trust and living up to this high standard. Our economic, education, political and religious systems require freedom to function. Without trust we have very few freedoms and our systems will not function properly. New systems can be created but they must be built on trust or we inevitably will lose freedom.

We're only human beings so perfection is unattainable. However we must try. We need to aim high.

And to be successful we need to C.A.R.E.

Appendix: Bonus Material

The following are various links to different resources that are available that can help you develop skills that will improve your career and life.

For <u>bonus material</u> from this book please visit:
<u>https://theconsultingplaybook.com/bonus</u>

To access detailed instructions on developing your values and principles please go to:
<u>https://theconsultingplaybook.com/values</u>

To develop or improve consulting skills please visit:
<u>https://theconsultingplaybook.com/successcode</u>

To develop more <u>skills related to trust</u> please go to:
<u>https://theconsultingplaybook.com/trustcourse</u>

For skills related to better <u>managing meetings</u> please go to:
<u>https://theconsultingplaybook.com/effectivemeetings</u>

For <u>coaching or mentorship</u> please go to:
<u>https://theconsultingplaybook.com/coaching</u>

To purchase a copy of <u>The Consultant's Code</u> please go to:
<u>The Consultant's Code</u>

Acknowledgments

I would like to express my gratitude to the many people who helped me throughout the writing of this book. Thank you to the many mentors who provided me advice over the years. I appreciate all of my clients that provided opportunities for me to work with them.

Thank you to my editor, Chantel Hamilton, for guiding me through the process of completing this book.

Thank you to my parents, who supported and encouraged me throughout my life as well as my siblings Margie, Melissa, Ben and Tim for helping with this book and always being there for me.

I also want to acknowledge and thank the following people who provided a review or input to the book, Kristen Michalko, Gopal Singh, Guy Dowhy and Catherine Lam.

Above all, thank you to my wife, Bridget, for your support throughout my career, as well as to my son, Adam, and daughter, Zoe.

Sources

Chapter 2

Kouzes, James M. and Barry Z. Posner, 2011. Credibility: How Leaders Gain and Lose It, Why People Demand It. Hoboken, NJ: Jossey-Bass.

Kouzes, James M,1995. Achieving Credibility: The Key to Effective Leadership. Chicago: Nightingale-Conant.

Hovland, C. I., Lumsdaine, A. A., & Sheffield, F. D., 1949. Experiments on mass communication. Princeton, NJ: Princeton University Press.

Hovland, C., & Weiss, W., 1951. The influence of source credibility on communication effectiveness. The Public Opinion Quarterly.

http://www.credibilityinstitute.com

Petty, R.E.; Cacioppo, J.T, 1986. The Elaboration Likelihood Model of Persuasion. In Advances in Experimental Social Psychology, Berkowitz, L., Ed., New York: Academic Press.

Chaiken, S, 1980. Heuristic Versus Systematic Information processing and the use of source versus message cues in persuasion. Journal of Personality and Social Psychology,

Chen, S., & Chaiken, S., 1999. The Heuristic-Systematic Model in its Broader Context. In S. Chaiken & Y. Trope

(Eds.), Dual-Process Theories in Social Psychology. New York: Guilford Press.

Strenthal, Brian and Lynn W. Phillips and Ruby Dholakia. (1978). The Persuasive Effect of Source Credibility: A Situational Analysis. The Public Opinion Quarterly.

Sundar, Shyam S, Anne Oeldorf-Hirsch and Amulya K. Garga, 2008. A Cognitive-Heuristics Approach to Understanding Presence in Virtual Environments. CLEUP Cooperativa Libraria Universitara Padova.

Chapter 3

Burt, Micheal, 2017. Person of Interest: Become the Person Other People Want a Piece of and Can't Live Without.

Kouzes, James M. and Barry Z. Posner, 2011. Credibility: How Leaders Gain and Lose It, Why People Demand It. Hoboken, NJ: Jossey-Bass.

Demers, Jayson, 2015. 7 Strategies for Making Objective Decisions. Inc.

https://www.inc.com/jayson-demers/7-strategies-for-making-objective-decisions.html

Fry, Andy, 2017. The Consultant's Code: Four Pillars to Success in Your Career and Life. Scottsdale, AZ: Vantage Point Publishing.

Fuler, Buckminster, 1982. Critical Path, Estate of R. Buckminster Fuller.

Chapter 5

Deci, Edward and Richard M. Ryan, 2000. Self-Determination Theory and the Facilitation of Intrinsic Motivation, Social Development, and Well-Being. American Psychology.

Kernis, Michael and Brian Goldman, 2006. A Multicomponent Conceptualization of Authenticity: Theory and Research. Amsterdam: Elsevier.

Germeijs, Veerle and Paul de Boeck, 2002. A Measurement Scale for Indecisiveness and its Relationship to Career Indecision and Other Types of Indecision. European Journal of Psychological Assessment.

Rassin, Eric, 2007. A Psychology Theory of Indecision. Netherlands Journal of Psychology.

Chapter 6

Wilmington, Ron, 2003. Authenticity: The Head, Heart, and Soul of Selling, New York: Doubleday.

Chapter 8

Kececioglu, Dimitri B, 2003. Maintainability, Availability, and Operational Readiness Engineering Handbook, Lancaster, PA: DesTech Publications.

Kouzes, James M. and Barry Z. Posner, 2011. Credibility: How Leaders Gain and Lose It, Why People Demand It. Hoboken, NJ: Jossey-Bass.

Price, Paul Christopher, Rajiv Jhangiani, and I-Chant A. Chiang, 2014. Research Methods in Psychology. BCcampus, BC Open Textbook Project.

Project Management Institute, 1992. Project & Program Risk Management. Newtown Square, PA: Project Management Institute.

Chapter 9

Pew Research Center, 2019. NonBook Readers Methodology. Pewresearch.org.

National Endowment for the Arts, 2008. Reading on the Rise. Washington, DC: National Endowment for the Arts.

Chapter 11

Nowak, Martin and Roger Highfield, 2011. SuperCooperators: Altruism, Evolution, and Why We Need Each Other to Succeed. New York: Free Press.

Goron, R.H., 2010. SITUATIONAL EMPATHY AND BEHAVIORAL EMPATHY, University Paris Nanterre.

Zillmann, Dolf, 2006. Empathy: Affective Reactivity to Others' Emotional Experiences. In J. Bryant & P. Vorderer (Eds.), Psychology of entertainment). Lawrence Erlbaum Associates Publishers.

Goldman, Alvin, 2012. Theory of Mind. Oxford Handbook of Philosophy and Cognitive Science. Oxford, England: Oxford University Press.

Emoto, Masaru, 2004. The Hidden Messages in Water, Hillsboro, OR: Beyond Words Publishing.

Fehr, Ernst and Klaus M. Schmidt, 1999. A Theory of Fairness, competition and Cooperation. The Quarterly Journal of Economics. Oxford, England: Oxford University Press.

Chapter 12

Tartakovsky, Margarita, 2018. Therapists Spill: 12 Ways to Accept Yourself. PsychCentral.

DiPirro, Danielle, 2013. Stay Positive: Daily Reminders from Positively Present. Positively Present Media.

Fletcher, Susan, 2014. "5 Strategies to Help Cope with Compassion Fatigue." Scrubs. August 15. http://scrubsmag.com/you-can-cope-with-compassion-fatigue/

About the Author

Andy Fry has worked in the consulting industry since 1997, and as an information technology (IT) consultant since 1998. As a CMA, CPA, and PMP, Andy has helped many companies through their IT implementations and business-improvement initiatives.

Andy is the international best-selling author of *The Consultant's Code: Four Pillars to Success in Your Career and Life.* In 2008, Andy founded Quantas Consulting Corp., a consulting company focused on helping clients with their Oracle Applications and tools (quantasconsulting.com). He also runs the website The Consulting Playbook (theconsultingplaybook.com), which is a platform that allows him to share his knowledge and experience with other consultants by providing education and training.

He is also a co-founder, co-host, and contributor to the "Art of Consulting Podcast", a podcast that provides information and education to consultants. Andy believes that human beings have built-in capabilities to achieve greatness and he wants to share his skills to see others achieve their potential.

He's grateful for all of the support and advice he has received over the years from his family, friends, and colleagues. He lives in Scottsdale, Arizona, with his wife and two children.

Your Personal Notes

"Acquiring the habit of note-taking is a wonderfully complimentary skill to that of listening."
-Richard Branson